PAINTING

INTERIOR AND EXTERIOR PAINTING STEP BY STEP

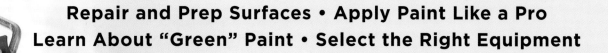

Repair and Prep Surfaces • Apply Paint Like a Pro
Learn About "Green" Paint • Select the Right Equipment

THUNDER BAY
P·R·E·S·S

San Diego, California

Thunder Bay Press
An imprint of Printers Row Publishing Group
10350 Barnes Canyon Road, Suite 100, San Diego, CA 92121
www.thunderbaybooks.com

Printers Row Publishing Group is a division of Readerlink Distribution Services, LLC.

Thunder Bay Press is a registered trademark of Readerlink Distribution Services, LLC.

All notations of errors or omissions should be addressed to Thunder Bay Press, Editorial Department, at the above address. All other correspondence (author inquiries, permissions) concerning the content of this book should be addressed to Creative Homeowner, *www.creativehomeowner.com*, 903 Square Street, Mount Joy, PA 17552.

Thunder Bay Press
Publisher: Peter Norton
Associate Publisher: Ana Parker
Publishing/Editorial Team: April Farr, Kelly Larsen, Kathryn C. Dalby
Editorial Team: JoAnn Padgett, Melinda Allman, Dan Mansfield

Creative Homeowner
Author: John D. Wagner
Photography: John Puleio
Junior Editor: Jennifer Calvert
Editorial Assistant: Sara Markowitz
Photo Coordinator: Robyn Poplasky
Indexer: Schroeder Indexing Services
Digital Imaging Specialist: Frank Dyer

Library of Congress Cataloging-in-Publication data is available upon request.

ISBN: 978-1-64517-097-6

Printed in China

23 22 21 20 19   1 2 3 4 5

Photo Credits

All photography by John Puleio/CH except where noted.

page 10: *top right* iStockphoto.com/Diane Diedrich; *bottom* iStockphoto.com/Jason Cheng; *top left* iStockphoto.com/Jan Pietruszka **page 15:** davidduncanlivingston.com **page 16:** Eric Roth **page 17:** *top right* Steven Miric/iStockphoto.com; *bottom* Eric Roth; *top left* Dan Epstein, color consultant: Amy Wax/Your Color Source Studios, Inc. **page 18:** *left* iStockphoto.com; *right* Pippa West/iStockphoto.com **page 19:** James Boulette/iStockphoto.com **page 20:** Jessie Walker **page 21:** *right* Phillip H. Ennis Photography **page 22:** *top left* courtesy of Werner Ladder **page 25:** courtesy of Georgia Pacific **page 26:** *left* Brian C. Nieves/CH; *right* John Parsekian/CH **page 27:** *left* courtesy of Helios **page 29:** *bottom right* John Parsekian/CH **page 30:** *bottom both* Brian C. Nieves/CH **page 31:** courtesy of Werner Ladder **page 35:** courtesy of Wagner Spray Tech Corp. **pages 37–39:** *all* courtesy of Werner Ladder **page 42:** *top right* John Parsekian/CH; *top left* courtesy of Chesney's Inc. **page 45:** *bottom right* courtesy of Werner Ladder **pages 47–51:** *all* John Parsekian/CH **page 53:** *all* John Parsekian/CH **pages 62–63:** *all* John Parsekian/CH **pages 70–71:** John Parsekian/CH **page 72:** *top right & center right* John Parsekian/CH; *bottom right* Mike Clarke/iStockphoto.com; *top left* courtesy of Werner Ladder **page 74:** *bottom right* Donald R. Swartz/iStockphoto.com **page 75** *bottom left* Christopher Badzioch/iStockphoto.com **page 77:** John Parsekian/CH **page 79:** John Parsekian/CH **page 80:** *bottom left* John Parsekian/CH **page 88:** *both* courtesy of Werner Ladder **page 91:** Lisa F. Young/iStockphoto.com **page 92:** *top right* John Parsekian/CH; *bottom right* iStockphoto.com; Andrew Hill/iStockphoto.com **page 94:** *bottom right* courtesy of GarageTek **page 96:** *bottom right* Jim Roberson/CH **page 97:** *all* John Parsekian/CH **page 98:** *left* Michael Westhoff/iStockphoto.com; *right* iStockphoto.com

Shutterstock credits: **page 1:** Syda Productions **pages 2-3:** alessandro guerriero **page 4:** N_Sakarin **page 7:** Mega Pixel **page 11:** *top* Andriy Blokhin *bottom* Sashkin **page 12:** Bukhta Yurii **page 23:** *top* OlegDoroshin *bottom* CandyBox Images **page 24:** Flegere **page 43:** *top* Photographee.eu *bottom* Africa Studio **page 44:** Africa Studio **page 73:** *bottom right* Robynrg *bottom left* notYourBusiness *top* Africa Studio **page 93:** *top* ronstik *bottom right* Brilliant Eye *bottom left* J. Bicking **page 101:** *top left* Maggie P *top right* Lolostock *bottom* serato **page 102:** Dan Dragos

contents

safety first

Though all the designs and methods in this book have been reviewed for safety, it is not possible to overstate the importance of using the safest construction methods possible. What follows are reminders; some do's and don'ts of basic carpentry. They are not substitutes for your own common sense.

always

■ *Always* use caution, care, and good judgment when following the procedures described in this book.

■ *Always* be sure that the electrical setup is safe; be sure that no circuit is overloaded and that all power tools and electrical outlets are properly grounded. Do not use power tools in wet locations.

■ *Always* read container labels on paints, solvents, and other products; provide ventilation, and observe all other warnings.

■ *Always* read the manufacturer's instructions for using a tool, especially the warnings.

■ *Always* use hold-downs and push sticks whenever possible when working on a table saw. Avoid working short pieces if you can.

■ *Always* remove the key from any drill chuck (portable or press) before starting the drill.

■ *Always* pay deliberate attention to how a tool works so that you can avoid being injured.

■ *Always* know the limitations of your tools. Do not try to force them to do what they were not designed to do.

■ *Always* make sure that any adjustment is locked before proceeding. For example, always check the rip fence on a table saw or the bevel adjustment on a portable saw before starting to work.

■ *Always* clamp small pieces firmly to a bench or other work surface when using a power tool on them.

■ *Always* wear the appropriate rubber or work gloves when handling chemicals, moving or stacking lumber, or doing heavy construction.

■ *Always* wear a disposable face mask when you create dust by sawing or sanding. Use a special filtering respirator when working with toxic substances and solvents.

■ *Always* wear eye protection, especially when using power tools or striking metal on metal or concrete; a chip can fly off, for example, when chiseling concrete.

■ *Always* be aware that there is seldom enough time for your body's reflexes to save you from injury from a power tool in a dangerous situation; everything happens too fast. Be *alert!*

■ *Always* keep your hands away from the business ends of blades, cutters, and bits.

■ *Always* hold a circular saw firmly, usually with both hands so that you know where they are.

■ *Always* use a drill with an auxiliary handle to control the torque when large-size bits are used.

■ *Always* check your local building codes when planning new construction. The codes are intended to protect public safety and should be observed to the letter.

never

- *Never* work with power tools when you are tired or under the influence of alcohol or drugs.

- *Never* cut tiny pieces of wood or pipe using a power saw. Cut small pieces off larger pieces.

- *Never* change a saw blade or a drill or router bit unless the power cord is unplugged. Do not depend on the switch being off; you might accidentally hit it.

- *Never* work in insufficient lighting.

- *Never* work while wearing loose clothing, hanging hair, open cuffs, or jewelry.

- *Never* work with dull tools. Have them sharpened, or learn how to sharpen them yourself.

- *Never* use a power tool on a workpiece—large or small— that is not firmly supported.

- *Never* saw a workpiece that spans a large distance between horses without close support on each side of the cut; the piece can bend, closing on and jamming the blade, causing saw kickback.

- *Never* support a workpiece from underneath with your leg or other part of your body when sawing.

- *Never* carry sharp or pointed tools, such as utility knives, awls, or chisels, in your pocket. If you want to carry such tools, use a special-purpose tool belt with leather pockets and holders.

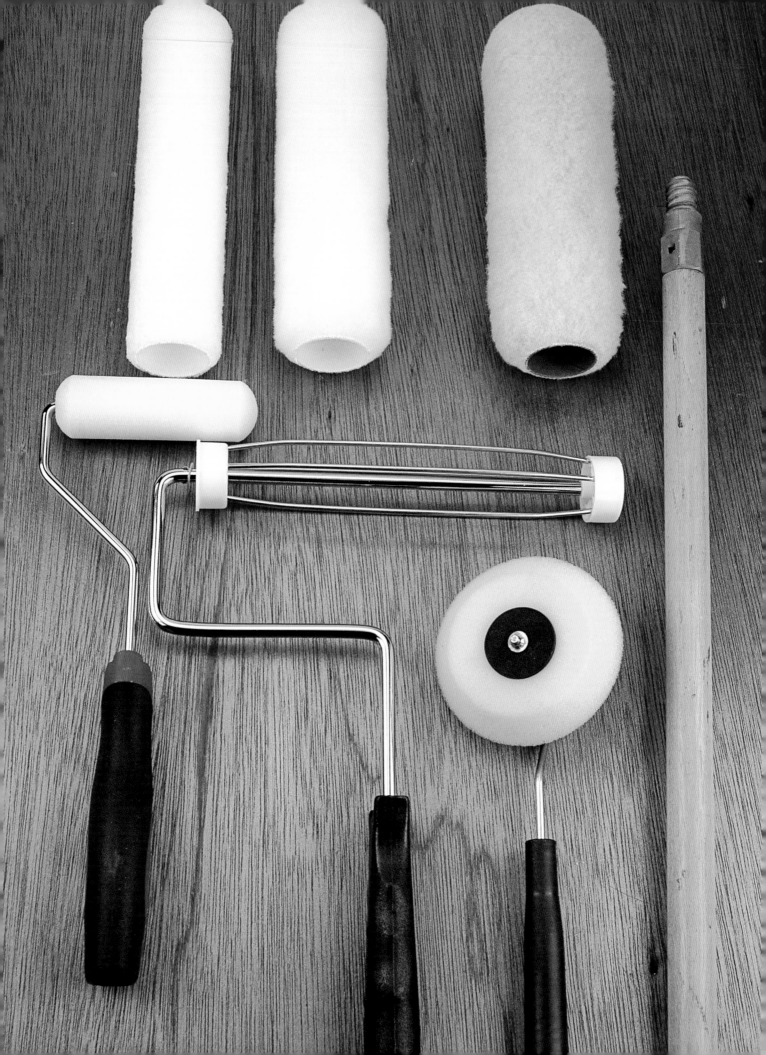

introduction

The Principles of Painting

Painting is the most popular project for do-it-yourselfer homeowners. People who panic when confronted with a stuck window or leaky faucet think nothing of picking up a paintbrush and changing the look of a room. Painting is easy to learn, requires inexpensive equipment, and for the most part is safe—although you will see there are necessary precautions to take in certain situations. To many people, the toughest part of painting is picking the right color. But being easy does not automatically lead to great-looking paint jobs. As with any project, professional-quality results come with proper preparation, the right materials, and good technique.

Painting provides the necessary information to help you do the job right. Beginning with a chapter on picking the right color palette for the interior and exterior of your house, the book moves to selecting the paint and materials you will need for the job. From there *Smart Guide: Painting* shows you the professional way to paint—how to prepare the surfaces you will paint, how to use a paintbrush and roller correctly, and how to approach the project in an efficient, organized manner.

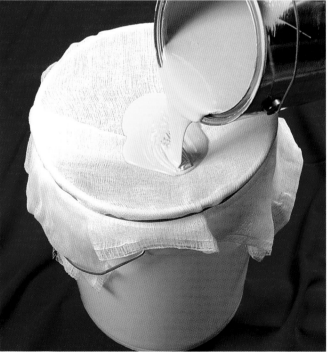

color basics

Picking Colors

The process of picking paint colors for your home may seem totally subjective—you simply pick the colors you like. That is only partly true. While it makes sense to start with the colors you like, other elements come into play. For example, do the colors you've selected work well together? Do they work with furnishing, carpeting, and window treatments already in place? Picking paint colors is really part art, part science. Let's start with the science part.

The Color Wheel

The color wheel arranges the color spectrum in a circle. It is a good way to see which colors work well together. It includes primary colors (red, blue, and yellow), secondary colors (green, orange, violet), and tertiary colors (red-blue, blue-red, and so on). Secondary colors are made by mixing two primaries together, such as blue and yellow to make green. A primary color, such as blue, and a secondary color, such as green, can be mixed to make a tertiary color—in this case, turquoise.

Now that you've got a color wheel in front of you, use it to help you envision certain color combinations. An analogous scheme involves neighboring colors that share an underlying hue.

Complementary colors lie opposite each other on the color wheel and often work well together. For instance a red and green living room in full intensity might be hard to stomach, but consider a rosy pink room with sage green accents. The same complements in varying intensities can make attractive, soothing combinations. A double complementary color scheme involves an additional set of opposites, such as green-blue and red-orange.

Color Wheel Combinations

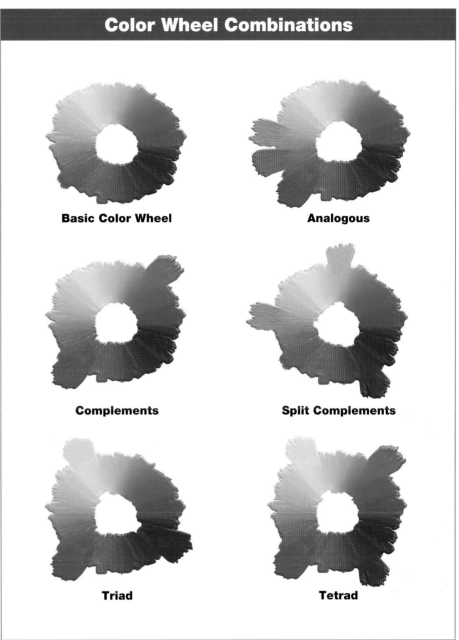

Basic Color Wheel

Analogous

Complements

Split Complements

Triad

Tetrad

Alternatively, you could go with a monochromatic scheme, which involves using one color in a variety of intensities. This ensures a harmonious color scheme. When developing a monochromatic scheme, lean toward several tints or several shades, but avoid too many contrasting values—that is, combinations of tints and shades. This can make your scheme look uneven.

If you want a more complex palette of three or more colors, look at the triads formed by three equidistant colors, such as red/yellow/blue or green/purple/orange. A split complement is composed of three colors—one primary or intermediate and two colors on either side of its opposite. For example, instead of teaming purple with yellow, shift the mix to purple with orange-yellow and yellow-green.

Lastly, four colors equally spaced around the wheel, such as yellow/green/purple/red, form a tetrad. If such combinations sound a bit like Technicolor, remember that colors intended for interiors are rarely undiluted. Thus yellow might be cream; blue-purple, a dark eggplant; and orange-red, a muted terra-cotta or whisper-pale peach. With less jargon, the color combinations fall into these two basic camps:

■ **Harmonious, or analogous, schemes,** derived from nearby colors on the wheel—less than halfway around.

■ **Contrasting, or complementary, schemes,** involving directly opposite slices of the pie.

Interior Colors

Don't just choose one color; think in terms of picking a color scheme. Survey your furniture, curtains, window treatments, and carpets, and note which colors might complement them.

Next make note of how many colors you think you might be using. Will the baseboard be a different color than the walls? It usually is, unless the trim is in bad shape and you don't want to call attention to it. The same is true of other trim, such as window casings and chair rail.

How about where the walls meet the ceiling? Will you install crown molding or some other type of cornice treatment there? Or will you be painting the walls and demarcating the ceiling-wall junction with a color change?

In addition to paint colors, you will also need to determine the level of finish or sheen the paint will have. The choices range from the most shiny—high gloss and semigloss—to the dullest—eggshell and flat. These designations vary with paint manufacturer, but they are important because the sheen of paint affects the color. There is more on this subject in Chapter 2, but a rule of thumb states that walls usually receive flat or eggshell finishes, whereas ceilings are almost invariably painted with a flat finish. Trim is typically painted with a semigloss or high gloss. These finishes are more durable and easier to clean than duller finishes.

Think in terms of groups of colors. Paint manufacturers group like colors together, below.

Colors change under different types of light, opposite. Examine samples under varying conditions.

Interior Walls

All paint stores can provide color chips of the paints they sell. Color chips will give you a small-scale idea of what the colors will look like once applied. You will need to do more than look at color chips to get a true sense of your colors, but they are a good place to start. In fact, a seasoned sales person at your local paint store can help you select color chips in a scheme. If you choose a buttercup yellow for the walls, the sales person can suggest color chips that are typically associated with a scheme that has buttercup yellow as its anchor color.

When you have whittled down your color choices, look at the color chips, or swatches, in different types of light, including natural light at different times of the day and in varying levels of artificial light. Even then, this color chip process is just to get an idea of paints that you will sample in larger swaths of color. Very few professional designers pick from chips, even though they may start their color selection from chips. If they do examine chips, they examine them one at a time on a white background.

Color Changes. Keep in mind that large surface areas make any paint color appear darker than the color chip. The degree of variation is usually equal to two shades. If you pick the color chip you desire, step "back" two shades darker for a true representation of what the color will look like when dry. Also, paint always looks darker once it dries. So, when you finally apply the paint, don't panic if the color doesn't look right at first. Wait until it dries. (Only then would it be perfectly OK for you to panic if you are surprised at the results.)

When you are zeroing in on your final colors, paint a 2 x 3-foot posterboard or cloth with the anchor color, and place it around the house so that you can see it in different light and near different colored carpets and furniture.

Color and Room Size. Colors can affect the way you perceive the size of a room. Warm colors like reds, yellows, and oranges will make a space seem smaller because they can provide a cozy feeling to the space. The so called cool colors like blues and greens appear to recede from you, making a room appear larger than it really is. If you really want to make a room seem large, go with an old standby such as a shade of white—there are dozens—or a neutral color.

Sizing the Room

As you get closer to buying paint, determine the square footage of the area you will paint. Multiply the length of each wall by the width. Subtract the area occupied by the doors, windows, and other openings. Add all of the measurements together to get a total square footage of the surface you must paint. If you are applying two coats, which is normal for most paint jobs, you will be painting the area twice.

Trimwork

The molding and trimwork around windows, doors, baseboards, chair rails, and cornices, offer the opportunity to add additional color to a room. In many cases, the trimwork is painted a color that complements the color used on the walls, creating a framing effect. Another option is to use a color in the same family as the color used on the walls but in a darker or lighter shade. A light-color wall with a slightly darker trim accentuates the decorative elements in the room.

Paint tends to dry darker than it appears on the paint chip, opposite.

Contrasting trimwork, right, frames the flat wall surfaces.

Use furniture and carpeting, far right, as cues for selecting paint colors.

A light-colored ceiling, below, makes a room appear larger.

Ceilings

Once you have settled on a wall color, move on to the ceiling. A traditional ceiling color is white with a flat finish. The flat finish will avoid a distracting sheen affect that can occur with glossy ceiling treatments,

and a white ceiling makes the room look expansive. In the same way that dark wall colors make a room look smaller, dark ceilings seem to shrink a room. A dark ceiling will make the room feel enclosed and small. If you are going for a cozy feel to the room, then dark colors may be preferred. Finally, note that a flat finish doesn't just avoid the sheen across the ceiling, but a flat finish can help hide imperfections and cracks in the ceiling surface, which a gloss or semi-gloss surface would highlight.

Exterior Colors

As with interiors, it is best to think in terms of groups of colors rather than single colors. But the task is often more complicated because houses are often built of a variety of materials that all have different textures, such as wood clapboard siding paired with a stone foundation or a brick building with wood trim. If you want to emphasize the difference in textures, paint each element a different color.

The Big Picture

When picking colors, note that two colors that may work well together as a siding and trim combination may clash with the roof color or some other element, such as the deck or landscaping. So when picking colors, remember to factor in things you can't, or won't, change, such as roofing material, the nearby landscape and plantings, any masonry work, and the color of your neighbors' houses.

PRO TIP

There are many online paint planning programs. Leading paint manufacturers such as Benjamin Moore (www.benjaminmoore.com), Valspar (www.valsparatlowes.com), Glidden (www.glidden.com), and Sherwin Williams (www.sherwin-williams.com) feature paint color planners online. Simply search "virtual paint color planner" on the Internet for a list.

Local Customs. When deciding on a house color, consider the local customs in your town. It is increasingly common for towns and communities to insist on some control over house colors. For example, in the resort community of Hilton Head, South Carolina, residents must choose exterior colors from a limited palette of muted shades (even the stop signs have color restrictions), whereas in the city of Charleston, there is a well-known district of pastel-colored houses called "Rainbow Row" where bold colors are welcome. Some planned communities can even fine you or make you repaint your home you don't use one of the accepted paint colors.

Testing Color Schemes. As with the interior color selection process, you can start deciding on color placement without actually painting anything. Trace or sketch a line drawing of your house, and then make several photocopies to try different schemes. Using a pencil or highlighter, shade different features and experiment with high-lighting possibilities. Decide which features you would like to

Highlight ornate trimwork, below left, with eye-catching colors.

Traditional shutters, below right, are usually painted a dark color.

PRO TIP

A great way to look at how colors work together is to see them in fabrics. Fabrics are often designed by people who study color and have worked with it for a long time. The microcosm of a couch-and-pillow combination in a popular catalog may hold the color scheme that will make your home look spectacular.

Consider roof color, masonry surfaces, and landscaping, below, when selecting an exterior color scheme for your home.

Pre-fab Color Schemes

Deciding on the specific colors in a multicolor scheme is a little tricky. It's the reason that almost all of the major paint companies have created "combo cards" to help you to pick body, trim, and accent colors in one step. These colors are also available in historic shades designed to match the most prevalent color schemes of certain periods. One nice feature of these cards is that the trim and accent color chips often overlap the body color, which helps demonstrate a more realistic relationship.

emphasize and which ones you would like to hide. The goal here is to create a well-balanced whole where no element seems to dominate. By "pre-painting" in this manner, you will not only avoid any disappointment, you'll be encouraged to try some distinctive schemes before you pick up the paintbrush.

Also, some paint stores have computers that will "paint" your house for you right on the computer screen. The better systems are equipped to scan a high-quality photo of your home. Or you can provide a high-resolution digital image.

Even if you are not able to get an exact reproduction of your house, these programs will give you a sense of what sorts or combinations are pleasing and demonstrate some ideas of how you might paint.

Down to Basics

Now that you have selected the colors for your home, it's time to decide which colors should be assigned to specific architectural elements. Generally the siding is done in one color, but if there is decorative molding above the first floor, a second color siding can be very interesting. Casings around windows and doors should all be the same color or the house will seem too busy. If there are decorative highlights in your trim and molding, two or more colors are fine if the pattern repeats on the whole structure. Some Victorian homes can look balanced with six colors, so there is no firm rule.

One common fashion is to paint the window sash and trim a color that is lighter than the body of the house. Shutters, if present, are usually painted darker than the house body. Of course, fashions change. For example, at the turn of the century, gloss black was the most popular choice for the window sash. But you rarely see gloss black today except on shutters.

Here's some tips for other architectural highlights:

Front Entrance. Create a striking effect by adding an accent color to this important element of your home. For example, a white house with a door painted a bright color, such as red or green, draws attention to the door making the entrance seem more inviting.

Frieze. A historically appropriate treatment for the frieze is to use both the trim and body colors. Let the trim color be the dominant one to mark a clear distinction from the top of the siding. Be careful not to introduce too many colors; you could end up with an effect that is too busy.

Corner Brackets. Brackets need to be perceived as part of the overall structure and should be painted so as not to appear that they are "floating free" of the structure. Use the principle trim color. Avoid using too much color. Some painters add a leading edge of scarlet to these features.

Sandwich brackets are a little different. Because they consist of more than one layer and are more complex than simple corner brackets, it is more acceptable to use several colors. Paint the exterior pieces to match the trim and frieze, and the center another color to show off your scroll work.

Posts. If you have simple rectangular wooden posts on a porch, you probably don't want to emphasize them with their own color. Paint them to match either the overall trim or body paint of your house. However, if your posts have special millwork, such as a chamfer on a square post or a ring on a turned post, it is perfectly acceptable to highlight these decorations with a flourish.

Many people like to paint porch ceilings sky blue, below, because they say the color mimics nature. These white columns add a nice contrasting touch.

Rails. The rails are essentially extensions of the posts. Therefore, they are usually painted in the same color as the posts.

Balusters. Try painting the balusters a lighter color than the rails. If the posts and rails have been treated in the main body color, try using the trim colors to make them stand out. Even if you have elaborately worked balusters, don't use too many colors to demonstrate your handiwork. Besides the amount of time that would be involved in detailing each baluster, the effect will look busy.

Floors and Ceiling. Porches are painted certain colors not only for decoration, but as matters of practicality. Light-colored ceilings maintain a sense of airiness and brightness. Painting porch ceilings blue is a technique that has been used for centuries to suggest the sky overhead and is rumored to keep nesting insects, such as wasps, from settling in. If the undersides of your porch ceiling rafters are exposed, you might paint them by using a combination of the body and trim colors. A dark floor is even more practical because it shows dirt and tracks less readily than a floor painted a lighter color.

Steps and Risers. The risers of wooden steps are normally painted the trim color, while the treads carry a surface (porch or deck) to the ground and should be painted in the same color. The handrail and balusters on the steps should be painted to match the porch rail and baluster color scheme.

Masonry Foundations. Many houses have a band of brick or concrete block below the siding. While it is fine to have this band the same color as the siding, a darker color makes the house seem firmly planted and will hide dirt and mud. Basement windows are generally painted the same dark color to de-emphasize them.

A bright accent color, below left, draws attention to this door.

Select a trim color, below right, that contrasts with the main color.

paint & tools

Latex versus Oil-Based Paints

The paint world is divided into two broad groups: latex, or water-based paints, and alkyd, or oil-based paints. (See "What's in Paint," right.) Homeowners and professional painters like latex paint because it dries in just a few hours and cleanup is easy. Quick drying allows the application of two coats in one day. When the job is done, everything can be cleaned with soap and warm water. To cleanup after painting with an oil-based product, you will need turpentine or mineral spirits. Latex paint is environmentally friendlier than its oil-based cousin. Unlike oil-based paint, latex emits little or no volatile organic compounds (VOCs), which are restricted in many states. VOCs create ground-level smog and can irritate the respiratory and cardiovascular systems. Compared with oil-based paint, latex paint is easier on the eyes, nose, lungs, and skin. It is also much more forgiving if you need to clean up a spill.

What's In Paint

There are three main ingredients in paint: binders, solvents, and pigment. Some paints contain additional additives.

Binders. When paint dries, it forms a film, and that film—the part of the paint that hardens—is called the binder. Binders include such things as acrylics, polyurethanes, oils, and latex. For oil-based paints, alkyd, linseed oil, and tung oil are common binders. Styrene acrylic, acrylic (a clear plastic), or vinyl acrylic (PVA) are the binders in water-based paints.

Solvents. Solvents are the liquids that float the solid into place where it can cure or dry. Solvents evaporate at room temperature, which means they are "volatile." Because they are compounds made from carbon atoms, they are called volatile organic compounds, or VOCs. Oil-based paints use petrochemicals as solvents, whereas latex uses a water-based emulsion.

Pigment. The pigment determines the texture, color, and covering capabilities of the paint. You can judge the quality of the paint by the texture of the pigment. Try rubbing a small sample of the paint between your fingers. If it feels milky and silky smooth, then the pigments are ground finely and you have a good-quality product. If the paint feels gritty, it contains a cheaper pigment.

Additives. Paint can have additional additives that enhance certain properties, such as flow, dry times, and thickness. Some of these products are available in small cans that you can add to the paint on your own.

PRO TIP

After using mineral spirits or turpentine to clean brushes, allow the cloudy liquid to settle overnight. The paint will end up on the bottom of the container, leaving perfectly good clear mineral spirits or turpentine to be poured off and used again.

The Pros' Choice. In the past, many professional painters resisted using latex paint, especially on woodwork or any area that would be subjected to a lot of cleaning and scrubbing. Oil-based paint is more durable than latex paint, and it settles as it dries, meaning that it produces a smooth finish without visible brush strokes.

However, legislation to reduce VOCs has directed paint manufacturers to put research money into latex paints. This has resulted in improved products that provide attractive long-lasting finishes. Today, many professional painters use oil-based paint only to prime or recoat old oil-based paint.

In the event you are applying two coats of paint, you have to wait at least overnight before recoating oil-based paint. This can be inconvenient, especially if you can only work on weekends. If the first coat isn't dry on Sunday, you'll wind up waiting a week to finish the job.

Most municipalities have strict rules regarding the disposal of leftover oil-based paints and the solvents needed to clean brushes and rollers, which means you may find yourself stuck with half-empty containers. You could end up paying to dispose of excess paint products the same way you would pay to dispose of toxic waste.

Where to Use Them. Don't apply latex paint over old oil paint, unless you carefully sand or chemically degloss oil-based surfaces before recoating in latex. On the other hand, it is perfectly fine to use an oil-based primer under latex paint. Some painters do this routinely because oil primer soaks into unpainted surfaces, while latex does not.

Choosing a Sheen

In addition to choosing the color and whether you want latex or oil-based paint, you also need to choose the degree of sheen you want. The range runs from flat to gloss. Most sheens are available for both latex and oil-based formulations.

The degree of sheen is determined by the proportion of binder in the paint. The binder determines the degree to which the paint is absorbed into the painted surface and how much pigment is left to form a film on the surface—the more binder, the less the absorption and the glossier the paint.

Flat or Matte. A low-gloss finish hides minor flaws in the surfaces you paint. Because the paint is slightly rough, flat paints do not take scrubbing as well as glossier finishes. Scrubbing flat paint tends to spread out the dirt, leaving a larger dirty spot.

Eggshell and Satin. This is glossier than flat paint, with slightly better abrasion resistance. Satin is glossier than eggshell.

Semigloss. Semigloss paints take scrubbing moderately well. They are available in latex or oil-based.

Gloss. This is the highest gloss classification. It is highest in binders and lowest in absorption. Gloss paints take scrubbing well and are easiest to clean. However, the glossier the paint, the more it highlights any flaws on the surface.

Enamel. Years ago, this term was synonymous with oil-based paint. These days, it is a loose term that refers to the glossiness of paint. The term is reliable only in that you can be reasonably sure that a paint labeled "enamel" is a semigloss or gloss paint. One manufacturer's enamel may be glossier than anothers.

Use a primer, below, to cover patches, unpainted drywall, and any wall area that is damaged.

Paint sheens, right, range from flat, which is the dullest, to high gloss, which is the shiniest.

Flat

Satin

Semigloss

Gloss

Choosing a Primer

Primer prepares the surface to receive the topcoat of paint. Some products seal the surface so that the paint is not absorbed; others provide the necessary adhesion so that the paint binds to the surface. Primers are available for exterior and interior applications, and in both oil- and water-based formulas.

In general, most experts favor oil-based primer for exterior wood, and latex primer for interior plaster and drywall.

Oil-based or alcohol-based primers are used to hide stains on interior surfaces, such as water stains and crayon marks, and to seal wood surfaces that contain tannins or knots that would otherwise bleed through the paint. Pigmented shellac has superior hiding power, and it dries in minutes. (For more on selecting primers, see "Picking a Primer," page 55.)

Caution: Use shellac primers in very well-ventilated areas.

PRO TIP

When using fast-drying primers, keep a bunch of small foam disposable brushes nearby, and use them exclusively to apply the primer. You will find that fast-drying primers will ruin traditional bristle or nylon brushes because they are impossible to clean after dipped in these primers.

Trimwork, below, is usually painted with a semigloss paint because the sheen protects the wood, making it easier to clean than a duller sheen.

The paint store should shake the paint can for you. But you will usually need to stir the paint, right, when you are ready to begin work.

2 Paint & Tools

Thinning and Straining Paint

As a general rule, you do not need to thin paint for a house-painting job. When you get the paint home from the store, it is already mixed properly. However, if you accumulate and store an inventory of paint, some of the paint's solvent is likely to evaporate and you will have to thin it before it can be used. Another circumstance in which you may have to thin paint is when you are working in hot, dry weather. The thinner helps to make the paint flow properly. A simpler solution, however, is to plan your projects for spring or fall when the weather is mild.

The type of thinner needed varies according to the type of paint used. Latex paints are thinned with water, oil-based paints are thinned with mineral spirits, turpentine, or brand-name thinners. Read the instructions on the paint can for specifics.

Mixing Paint. Have the paint dealer shake the paint before you take it home. Then mix the paint using a stir stick just before you begin work to ensure even color. To avoid spills, mix the paint in a bucket (not in the can), and be sure to get all the sediment out of the can because that is where the pigment settles. If using more than one can, experts recommend mixing all of the paint in a large bucket to ensure even color.

Straining Paint. There are two good reasons for straining older paint: to remove grit and paint that has hardened. Sometimes during a paint job (typically an exterior job), the brush

If you are using paint from a previously opened can, below, you may need to strain the paint through cheesecloth to remove grit.

picks up grit from the work surface and deposits it in the paint bucket. If this happens, the grit finds its way back onto your brush, causing streaks and skips as you apply the paint. If your brush gets gritty, pour the paint through a piece of cheesecloth or panty hose, and clean the brush.

Stains

Stains are essentially pigments dissolved in either an oil- or water-based solvent. When you want to enhance the natural wood grain, stain is the finish of choice.

Interior Stains. These stains come in many wood-tone colors. They are most typically used on interior woodwork and furniture. Interior stains are usually covered with a clear topcoat, such as varnish or polyurethane. In fact, you can now buy finishes that are a combination of stain and polyurethane.

Exterior Stains. These stains are essentially paints with reduced amounts of pigment, and they are used on solid wood and plywood siding. There are two types of exterior stains. *Semitransparent* stain adds color but reveals the grain. *Solid* stains obscure the grain but are thinner than paint. Because stains are thinner than paint, they soak into the wood. As a result, stain does not peel or crack the way paint does, and you can add new coats through the years without worrying about building up layers that eventually have to be stripped off. Another advantage is that stains do not require primer.

There is a downside to the reduced amounts of pigment in stains. Pigment plays a big part in resisting the weather and sunlight that break down paint. Houses that have been painted with semitransparent stains must be recoated more frequently than houses coated with solid stains. All stained houses must be recoated more frequently than painted houses. The more severe the weather conditions (heat, humidity, direct sun) in your part of the country, the less suitable exterior stain becomes for your home.

When painting, left, you'll find it easier to work from a small container rather than a full paint can.

Stains add some color, below, but they also let the natural beauty of the wood shine through.

Lead Paint

If you are working in an area with peeling and flaking paint, be aware that the paint may contain lead. Lead was a common element in paint until 1969, and it was an additive until 1978. Inhaling lead dust can lead to a number of illnesses, especially in the very young and the very old. Any house paint applied before the mid-1970s is likely to contain lead. Even paints applied into the mid-1980s may contain some lead because of this paint stayed in retailers' or painters' inventories for years.

Prep work that involves sanding or scraping paint that was applied before the mid 80s is likely to create lead-laced chips and dust. Consult with local building officials or an environmental engineer for advice on how best to deal with the paint. Search "lead abatement" on the Internet, or visit the EPA.gov site. Some states and municipalities have laws that require specific steps for lead abatement; many area require a seller notify a potential home buyer is lead paint is present.

The inhalation or ingestion of lead causes lead poisoning. Symptoms include, but are not limited to, aches and pains, fatigue, confusion, and irreversible brain and neurological damage. Simple, inexpensive kits that detect lead in paint are available in many hardware and home-center stores.

PRO TIP

When doing preparation work that may disturb lead paint, follow these common sense precautions:
- Keep children and pregnant women away from the work site dust.
- Hang polyethylene sheeting secured with duct tape in door and window openings to contain the lead dust.
- Clean up all dust and chips at the end of every work day. Wash work clothes every day. Change clothes, and shower before taking lunch or dinner breaks.
- Have your pediatrician check your child's lead level. This fairly simple and inexpensive test is a good idea whether you are working with lead paint or not.

Any surface painted before 1978 should be tested for lead paint, left. You'll find easy-to-use test kits at any paint store or home center.

Testing for Lead Paint

1. Follow the directions that come on the packaging of the lead-paint test kit. For this model, you simply scrape the surface to remove a little of the paint, apply an activator that comes in the kit, and dab with a cotton swab.

2. This kit contains a test card. Dab the wet cotton swab onto the spaces indicated in the directions. This will tell you the lead content of the area tested. If you do discover lead paint, take the necessary precautions before sanding the surface. In many cases, covering with a coat of unleaded paint is sufficient.

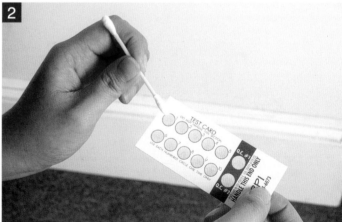

Green or Natural Paints

Paints produce VOCs, which are harmful to people. Combine that with tight-home construction where outdoor fresh air is limited due to energy concerns, and the typical weekend painting project can lead to health problems. Paint manufacturers have joined the "green revolution" by creating low- and no-VOC paints that cost about the same as non-green paints. There are three general types of green paint: natural paints, zero-VOC paints, and low-VOC paints.

Natural Paints. Natural paints are water-based products made from such ingredients as water, essential oils, clay, and even milk and milk-byproducts. Linseed oil and citrus oil are also used in some of the natural wood stains, oils, and waxes used for natural finishes on wood. These natural paint products could also be categorized as zero-VOC products because they do not off gas, unless you consider the smell of essential oils and citrus a product of off gassing. Search "natural paints" on the Internet.

Zero-VOC paints. The Environmental Protection Agency has set VOC limits for paint. To be considered a zero-VOC paint, it must contain less than 5 grams per liter.

Low-VOC Paints. Low-VOC paints and finishes are almost invariably water-based, and to meet the EPA standard that allows the use of the "low-VOC" label on the can, they must contain less than 250 grams per liter for latex paint and 380 for alkyd paint.

Certifying Paint

The Environmental Protection Agency has set national VOC standards, and any claims about VOCs should refer to those standards. But a number of private-sector building groups and trade groups have started certifying products. For paints, look for materials certified by the Greenguard, Green Seal, Scientific Certification Systems, or the Master Painters Institute's Green Performance Standards.

Paint manufacturers have lowered the levels of VOCs in their products. This is especially true of water-based paints.

Look for the zero-VOC designation on the paint label, below. Paints must meet standards of the EPA and are certified by independent groups.

Painting Tools

Choosing Tools

It is rare to come across a paint job that cannot be done quickly and efficiently with brushes and rollers, the meat and potatoes of painting tools. Brushes work well because they have narrow sides for narrow edges, broad sides for broad surfaces, and bristles that are flexible enought to fit into tight spots. A good-quality 3-inch tapered brush can handle almost any painting job.

When used on large flat areas, roller nap mimics brush bristles. Brush and roller technique comes naturally. People know almost instinctively which way to turn a brush or when a brush needs to be reloaded. It is easy to feel when a roller is skipping or pulling. If you buy the right brush-es and rollers and use them properly, they are all you need to apply the paint.

Choosing Brushes

The following brushes are useful for specific jobs.

Flat Brush. A 3- or 4-inch-wide brush with a tapered edge is the most common and most useful type of brush. It can cover large areas and produce sharp cut lines.

Sash Brush. This brush has angled bristles that are ideal for making crisp lines on trim, molding, and window muntins.

Stain Brush. The bristle area on this brush is shorter and wider than a

A good brush, below, has tapered bristles that won't pull free of the metal ferrule.

Types of brushes, opposite: synthetic flat and sash brushes, paint pads, and natural-bristle brush.

paint brush. This stubby design is meant to counteract the tendency stain has to drip into the brush ferrule (the metal band that holds the bristles in place).

Foam Brush. This tool consists of a foam pad on a stick. Its primary usefulness is that it is cheap and disposable. Some good foam brush jobs are applying stain or painting window trim (the tapered edge is the perfect size). Do not use foam brushes for applying paint remover because the foam will melt.

Rough-Surface Painter. This is a combination brush-and-paint-pad, and it's useful for painting rough surfaces such as exterior wood shingles. It looks like a scrub brush.

Selecting Bristles. There are two types of bristles from which to choose.

Nylon Bristles. These are best used for latex paint but they also can be used for oil-based paint.

Natural Bristle (also called China bristle). These brushes are preferred for use with oil-based paints and varnishes. They cost 40 to 50 percent more than synthetic-bristle brushes. Do not use natural-bristle brushes for latex paint. The water in the paint ruins the brush.

Testing a Brush. Before buying a brush, test it. Tug gently on the bristles. If more than a few pull out, do not buy the brush. Next, bounce and wiggle the bristles in your palm. A good brush has bristles that feel soft and springy, and that bounce back into shape quickly when you let go.

Make sure the bristles are thick and plentiful. Fold back the bristles with your hand, and look at where they connect to the handle. If you see a lot of handle between a few plugs of bristles you have an inferior brush. A good brush that is 1 or 2 inches wide has bristles that are about 3 inches long. A good brush that is 3 or 4 inches wide has bristles about 4 inches long.

Check the metal ferrule that holds the bristles to the handle. It must be substantial (not thin and flimsy) and firmly attached to the handle. Make sure it does not rock when the bristles are wiggled back and forth.

Choosing Rollers

The two parts to a paint roller include the handle (also called the frame or cage) and the furry cover, also known as a sleeve. Choose a good quality handle that feels comfortable in your hand and has some substance. Use the highest-quality covers.

To test a roller cover, roll the cover in your hand. The nap of a good roller has an even consistency, with no bumps or flat spots. Tug gently on the nap. If any fuzz comes off, find a better cover.

Nylon Roller Covers. These covers are suitable for most paint jobs. They are available in short, medium, and long-medium nap, and they are an appropriate choice for walls and ceilings. Long nap is especially suitable for painting concrete, brick, or other rough surfaces. Short nap can provide a smooth finish for very flat surfaces. Short nap covers hold relatively little paint, so more effort goes into frequent reloading of the roller and keeping a wet edge. Nylon covers can be stored wet from day-to-day during a paint job by wrapping them snuggly in a heavy garbage bag or in a plastic kitchen bag.

> ### PRO TIP
>
> Before using a roller cover, remove the lint (loose nap) with strips of masking tap, very much as you remove lint from a piece of clothing. This keeps the loose nap from coming off on the freshly painted wall.

Lamb's-Wool Covers. These are expensive, high-quality rollers. If you thoroughly clean and carefully dry a lamb's-wool cover, it can be used for many paint jobs. These covers produce a distinctive, slightly stippled effect. Some people like the finish, but others do not.

Doughnut Rollers. These small one-piece foam rollers are good for moldings and corners. Some painters find them indispensable, while others do every job with only brushes and a standard 9-inch roller. Small foam rollers are inexpensive, so try one.

Trim Rollers. These are useful for painting trimwork, cabinets, and vanities because of their size. They usually have a foam cover and do not leave a stipple like the rollers do.

Roller Pans. For interior work, choose a deep, sturdy metal roller pan. Stay away from flimsy metal and plastic pans. (Most shrink-wrapped kits consist of a poor-quality brush and roller in a cheap pan, and these do not provide good results.) At the store, pick up the pan and twist it. If it pops in and out of shape, do not buy it because the metal or plastic is too thin. In general, a deeper pan is best as it allows you to get more work done between refills.

Roller Screens. Rather than use a pan, consider a metal roller screen that fits into a large bucket. These are your best option for exterior work. Paint stores sell handy 2½-gallon square buckets that can hold a roller screen and have a lip for pouring paint back into a can. Because of their shape, they do not move or spin when hanging off a hook on the side of a ladder.

Extension Handles. For painting ceilings or exterior siding such as Texture 1-11 ("Tee one-eleven"), you need an extension handle for your roller. Many painters like to use an extension to minimize bending when rolling walls. You can keep the roller tray on the floor and step forward to move the roller on the wall. Some painters claim that using an extension handle on walls is easier on the shoulders. Unlike other equipment, you need not necessarily buy the best one you can afford. Some aluminum handles have a telescoping

> ### PRO TIP
>
> When cleaning a roller cover outdoors, use a hose with a spray nozzle. Hold the roller free in the air, and just catch the edge of one end of the roller cover with a stream of water. The roller will spin at a high rate of speed, throwing the paint off the cover.

Here is a variety of roller covers, roller frames, and an extension handle.

Paint holders include roller pan, bottom; bucket, and can with roller screens, top.

feature that allows you to adjust the length of the handle. Check the couplings on these models for smooth operation, and buy one that feels sturdy when extended.

Power Rollers. Power rollers are devices that pump paint from a can or reservoir through a specially made roller body. Most units will include paint pads as an accessory. The idea, which is a good one, is to eliminate the 50 percent of rolling time that a painter spends getting ready.

There are three types of power rollers commonly available. One employs a small dolly, which holds a can of paint and a pump. The dolly rides along behind you as you paint. The problem: it's pulled along by a hose, which can get in the way.

Another model power roller holds the paint in a reservoir, which you sling over your shoulder.

A third power roller sucks paint out of the can and into a long roller handle. You push the handle, like a syringe, to force paint into the roller.

Power rollers are for latex paint only. When you finish, hook up the pump to your utility-sink faucet or an outside hose faucet, and run water through the whole apparatus.

Power rollers can speed the work because there is no need to keep loading the roller. Some models have a carry-along paint supply; others have one that you pull along the floor.

Tips for Spraying

Here are a few tips to remember if you decide to use spray equipment to paint the siding:

■ Always wear eye and respiratory protection when spraying. The mist is fine and can be irritating and potentially harmful.

■ Be aware that tiny paint droplets are apt to drift in the air. They can land on neighbors' houses, cars, foliage, and driveways—causing big problems.

■ Never spray on windy days. When working on corners, spray vertically to avoid over-spray. Stop spraying about two feet short of all edges, and brush paint on the rest.

■ Good technique involves a steady wrist making quick and sure spray passes. Do not throw your arm out in an arc. Every sprayer concentrates the paint in the middle of the swath emitted so you must feather the edges of every pass.

■ Do not stop your hand or hold the trigger too long because too much paint will come out.

■ Most paint is too thick to pour directly from the can into the sprayer. Mix paint with an appropriate solvent (water or oil-based) to allow proper misting.

■ Never allow debris to get into the sprayer. The paint pot or connector tube must have a wire mesh cover to prevent objects from getting sucked in. When using previously opened paint, be sure to strain the paint through cheesecloth or panty hose to remove particles.

Paint Sprayers

There are three basic types of sprayers: high volume, low pressure; propulsion; and compressed air.

High Volume, Low Pressure (HVLP). This type of system atomizes paint. HVLP works well on small areas of interior surfaces, such as trimwork, cabinets, and louvered shutters. Models usually include different nozzles for different types of paint. Most manufacturers recommend thinning paint for ease of application.

Propulsion Sprayer. This type of machine is an electrically driven sprayer that flips or spits out small droplets of paint. In inexpensive models, the unit is fed by a small pot of paint. Those sprayers are excellent for small areas that are difficult to paint with a brush, such as louvered shutters or wicker furniture. More expensive models, generally used by professionals, have a hose that is connected to a large pail of paint and an adjustable rate of spray mist and pressure. These machines are excellent for spraying siding.

Compressed Air Sprayer. This type of sprayer is also electric. It emits a finer mist of paint that is driven by forced air shot through the paint. These units cover large surfaces with a smooth finish, but they are too expensive to justify for a single paint job. But they are widely available for rent.

PRO TIP

When spraying paint, use a flow-enhancement additive to help the paint move through the hose and nozzle. Flow enhancement additives may seem like just another extra the paint store is trying to sell you, but they really do make a difference in performance.

Nonpainting Tools

Most painting jobs require some sort of repair and prep work before you actually apply the paint. For these jobs, you will need an assortment of putty knives, paint scrapers, sandpaper, and sanding blocks, as well as spackle, drywall joint compound, and in some cases, epoxy wood fillers. Some tools can help you speed repair work. For example, if you are going to paint a room that has new drywall or if there are a number of drywall fixes, use a pole sander. The sander extends your arms so you can cover a large area while standing in one spot. It also extends your sanding stroke, making the sanded joints consistent.

Eye Protection. Wear goggles during sanding or scraping, or any other prep work that sends debris flying. In addition, paint flecks that fall into your eyes hurt, and cleaning oil paint out of lashes can be very unpleasant, so it is a good idea to wear safety glasses while painting (especially when using oil-based paint).

Ladders and Scaffolds

A great deal of painting takes place while standing on a ladder of some kind. As with any job, safety should be of paramount importance, especially when choosing, placing, and working from a ladder. There are three kinds of ladders: stepladders, fold-up (articulated) ladders, and extension ladders.

Stepladders. Stepladders are only stable on level surfaces. You should never use one on a slope. Plus, the higher you go, the more unstable the ladder becomes. If you find you're working with your feet on or near the top three steps, you should probably move to a scaffold, work platform, or extension ladder. A stepladder can be used for work up to 15 feet above the ground, depending on the size of your ladder.

When repainting, you will need putty knives and paint scrapers, left. The kit shown on the right of this photo contains different blades for different jobs.

Use sandpaper and sanding blocks, below left, to get a smooth finish to your repairs and patches.

A pole sander, below right, allows you to reach high up on the wall without leaving the floor.

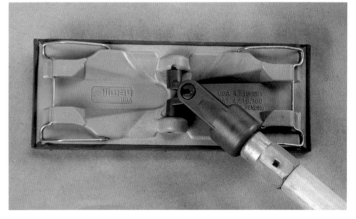

2 Paint & Tools

Articulating Ladders. Articulating, fold-up, ladders are ideal for working mid-distances, between 4 and 12 feet off the ground. These ladders are handy because you can configure them in different ways:

- Extend the ladder, and lock it straight to act as a standard, one-section ladder.
- Lock it in an "A" position to act as a stepladder.
- Place two together to form a sturdy base to support a work platform or low scaffold.

Extension Ladders. Extension ladders are used mostly for high outdoor work. Depending on the performance rating you use, these ladders can be quite sturdy and support the weight of a worker plus material (paint, tools, or one end of a plank). Extension ladders are available in a wide range of sizes, typically from 20 to 50 feet.

Ladder Materials. You'll find each kind of ladder in metal (usually aluminum) or fiberglass, and many stepladders and extension ladders are made of wood. The type you'll choose depends on the work you'll be doing and how much you want to spend.

Wooden Ladders. These ladders are not only heavy, but they also wear out, crack, and splinter with use. However, wooden ladders have two advantages: they are relatively inexpensive; and they do not conduct electricity, so they can be used when working around power cables.

Aluminum Ladders. Inexpensive and lightweight (depending on the grade), aluminum ladders are adequate for most jobs when you place them properly. The longer the ladder, the easier it is to use if it is aluminum. Most fold-up, or articulated, ladders are aluminum. Never use an aluminum ladder near wiring.

Fiberglass Ladders. If you're buying for a long-term investment, get a fiberglass ladder. It may cost more, but a top-of-the-line fiberglass ladder is extremely durable, strong, noncorrosive, and nonconductive.

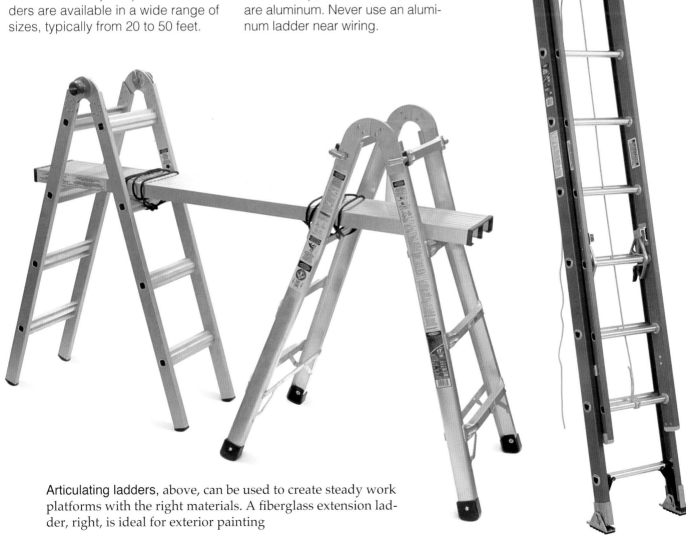

Articulating ladders, above, can be used to create steady work platforms with the right materials. A fiberglass extension ladder, right, is ideal for exterior painting

Ladder Ratings. Ladders are rated for the weight they can hold. You will see a sticker on most ladders identifying their "type." Type III ladders are light-duty and can carry 200 pounds per rung or step. Type II are medium-duty and can carry 225 pounds per rung or step. Type I ladders are heavy-duty industrial ladders and can hold 250 pounds per rung. Type IA ladders are extra heavy-duty and can hold 300 pounds per rung. For most painting jobs, a Type II ladder will serve your needs just fine.

Ladder Accessories

A *ladder stand-off* is a U-shaped bracket that attaches to the top of the ladder. Rather than have the side rails of the ladder in contact with the building, the stand-off is in contact. This allows you to set the ladder in the middle of a window so that you can reach the entire area. A *ladder leveler* consists of two legs that you can set to different heights. It allows you to have a stable ladder on a sloped surface. Don't use rocks, plywood, or scrap lumber to prop up a ladder's legs. It's unsafe.

A ladder leveler, left, allows you to work from a ladder on uneven surfaces.

All stepladders have a paint tray, but this one, below, has slots to hold different tools.

Often it is more practical to work from a platform rather than a ladder when painting. You can create a sturdy work platform using various kinds of brackets, called jacks, attached to a ladder, the roof, or 4x4 posts.

Ladder Jacks. These are nothing more than heavy metal brackets that hook onto ladders. Ladder jacks provide a stable, level place to hold 2x10 wood planks or an aluminum platform. To use the jacks, you need two ladders, one for each end of the plank or working surface. There are two kinds of ladder jacks: inside-bracket and outside-bracket types.

Inside ladder jacks suspend a plank or working platform beneath the ladders as they rest against a structure. Outside ladder jacks support a plank on the front face of the ladders as they rest against a structure. Either way, the jacks hook onto the rungs of the ladder or at the junction of rungs and rails.

Pump Jacks. Part of a system for lifting or lowering a work platform made of wood or metal planks, pump jacks are metal L-shaped brackets that travel up and down 4x4 or metal posts. The vertical part of the "L" hugs an upright, and the horizontal part supports a plank or working surface. Other brackets, which you attach to structural members such as rafters or studs, hold the uprights to the structure. To raise the working platform, you pump the L-shaped jacks with your foot. To lower the platform, you turn a crank.

A scaffold bracket turns an ordinary extension ladder into one leg of an extended work platform. Check code requirements in your area before using a scaffold.

Ladder standoffs put you in position to reach the entire window frame safely. No more reaching to the side to paint the middle of the window.

Work Lights

When painting indoors, work lights are essential, even if the room gets good daylight. The daylight will fade and change through the day, or it may be cloudy outside and the light inconsistent. Work lights come in a variety of sizes with different bulbs, which cast different types (and spectrums) of light.

Incandescent bulbs in a plastic or metal cage can serve most jobs very well. These are good tools to have in addition to other lighting solutions because you can use the light as a "wand" to move around and inspect the paint as it is applied.

If you need more light, try halogen lamps, which are very bright but give off a great deal of heat. Halogen lamps are often sold with an adjustable tripod-type stand so that you can stabilize the light source.

Fluorescent lights don't give off any heat, but they sometimes have a spectrum that can make colors look different from how they look in natural light. If you want to use a fluorescent light, look for one with a high color rendering index, or CRI, so the colors look as they will in daylight. Note that fluorescent lights, unlike halogen lights, can be entirely sealed against the weather and they last as much as 10 or 15 times longer than halogen bulbs.

Train dedicated work lights on your project as you work. Lights come with incandescent, fluorescent, or halogen bulbs. Lights on stands work best in an empty room.

Respirators

Even latex paint fumes can be irritating to eyes, nose, lungs, and skin. When painting inside, open enough windows to provide good cross-ventilation. For best ventilation, put a fan in a window and set it up so that it blows air out of the room. Wear a respirator if you are using a compressed-air spraying system. If you have heart or respiratory problems, consult a doctor before starting a prep or paint job. Wearing a respirator causes labored breathing and puts people with heart or respiratory problems at risk.

For paint removal and related work, you may need more than a nuisance-rated dust mask (a paper mask with one rubber band). When sanding, wear a respirator that is NIOSH-rated for dust and fibers, such as an N-95 mask.

Drywall and plaster dust can cause permanent damage to your bronchia and lungs. The best disposable dust masks have an exhalation valve that increases comfort.

If there is a chance of encountering asbestos (commonly used in buildings until the late 1970s), wear a half-mask respirator rated for asbestos. When working with coatings that produce fumes that may be toxic, which includes some lacquers and paint removers, wear a respirator that is NIOSH-rated for toxic fumes. The best respirators are reusable half-mask respirators, which include a set of prefilters in addition to the regular filters.

To be fully protected, above right, use a respirator, goggles, and no exposed skin.

When sanding, applying primers, paint strippers, and some paints, it is necessary to use some sort of mask. For light sanding, a plastic mask is usually sufficient, but for other jobs use a NIOSH-rated respirator.

chapter 3

interior painting

Getting Started

The key to a good paint job lies in preparation. About 80 percent of a painting job consists of prep work—moving furniture, protecting surfaces with drop cloths, patching damaged areas, and sanding—while only 20 percent of the work is applying paint. When the job is finished, the paint itself is not as noticeable as the care taken during the preparation work.

In a new house, wall and ceiling surfaces are usually in excellent condition, so you can expect to spend about two to three hours of prep time for every hour spent painting. On the other hand, in an older home, which most likely has some cracked plaster, damaged drywall, and built-up paint on the trim, it is not unusual to spend 8 to 10 hours prepping for every hour spent painting. If the job requires patching, plan ample drying time for spackle and joint compound.

If it is possible to remove all of the furniture from the room, do so. It is easier to move the furniture than it is to work around it. If some furniture must remain in the room, leave at least 4 feet of open space along the walls, and make sure you can reach the entire ceiling.

Removing Hardware. Doorknobs, escutcheons, window locks, and curtain rods must be removed. If the screws on any of this hardware are worn, now is the time to buy replacements. If standardized hardware, such as a window lock, is paint-encrusted or damaged, it might be easier to install replacement hardware than to clean up the existing material. However, you probably want to save and clean antique hardware if at all possible.

Covering Up. In most cases, you will not be able to remove everything from the room, so you must protect what is left. Place all movable furniture in the center of the room, and cover with canvas drop cloths. Don't be tempted to use newspaper because paint will leak through the paper. Cover hanging light fixtures in plastic. Remove door hardware. Mask the trim that you do not plan to repaint (such as baseboards, and door and window trim). Be sure to use painter's tape. Regular masking tape is too sticky and will remove finishes when you pull the tape off the surface.

Storing Hardware. Put the hardware in plastic bags so you do not lose or mix up parts. Use common masking tape to mask hardware that must stay in place (such as door hinges). Store small hardware in ziplock plastic bags. Label the bags.

Covering Ceiling Fixtures. Carefully mask ceiling fixtures. Put an old sheet or plastic sheeting over chandeliers and ceiling fans. It is much easier to paint the ceiling if you unscrew the ring at the top of the chandelier and allow the canopy to slide down toward the light.

Living Room Door

Prepainting Repairs

Walls and trimwork are subject to a variety of assaults that result in damage, especially in a house with children. Besides the everyday wear and tear that leads to scratches and gouges, walls also develop cracks as the house settles. Before beginning any paint job, study the surfaces carefully, and make the necessary repairs.

Minor Repairs

Filling Nailholes & Cracks. Fill nailholes and hairline cracks with drywall compound (often called drywall mud). Spackling compound is available in small containers, while drywall compound is generally available in quarts or five-gallon buckets. If the walls require minimal preparation (such as filling nailholes), choose a quick-drying spackling compound that has very little shrinkage and can be painted in as little as 10 to 15 minutes. Use a putty knife to apply either material. Sand smooth using 100-grit followed by 150-grit sandpaper when dry.

Cleaning Brass Hardware

Place hardware in an enameled pan with a solution of baking soda and water. Use about four tablespoons of baking soda per quart of water. Simmer the solution on top of a stove until the paint softens. Dump the hardware out of the pan, let it cool enough to touch, and then take off the paint with a stiff bristle brush toothbrush (not a wire brush). Polish the hardware with brass polish.

Fill small holes and cracks with drywall joint compound or any number of putty compounds. Use a putty knife to work the material into the damaged area.

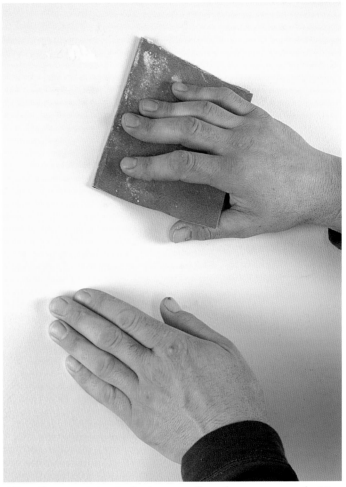

Allow the repair to dry before sanding the area smooth. Use a medium-grit sandpaper to remove most of the repair material. Follow with a fine-grit sandpaper.

Damaged Drywall Paper

The paper face of drywall can easily tear when you are prepping a room for painting, especially if you are stripping wallpaper, scraping loose paint, or even removing some sort of wall decoration. Here's how to repair the damage.

1 Remove the Damaged Material. Use a putty knife or a utility knife to cut the torn area away from the surface of the wall.

2 Fill the Depression. Spread a thin layer of drywall joint compound over the damaged area. It is best to overlap the repair area with the compound. For best results use a wide drywall knife rather than a putty knife.

3 Feather the Edge of the Repair. To make sure the spackling or drywall patch is not readily apparent, it must be "feathered." This term refers to the technique of tapering and sanding the edges of a patch into a very gradual slope. You will not feel a ridge at the edge of a patch that is properly feathered. Once the repair is smooth and blends with the surrounding wall, prime the patch before painting.

1 Tears in drywall paper need to be repaired before repainting. Begin by cutting away any hanging paper. Cut as much as is necessary to reach an undamaged area.

2 Apply a thin layer of drywall joint compound to the damaged areas. You won't need much material, but you should overlap the damaged area with the compound.

3 For unusually deep damage you may need to apply a second thin layer. When dry, sand the repair using sandpaper or a sanding block. Apply a primer to the repair before painting.

Major Repairs

To patch plaster walls, use drywall compound or patching plaster to patch small holes. While the methods for repairing minor flaws and nailholes are the same for both types of wall, the methods differ for bigger repairs. Holes in plaster that are no bigger than a fist can be patched with drywall compound, as long as the lath behind the hole is still intact. Repair larger areas with patching plaster.

Repairing Damaged Plaster

1 **Remove the Loose Plaster.** Get rid of any plaster that has lost its hold on the lath, but do not disturb undamaged plaster. To allow for a stronger patch, undercut the old plaster using a can opener. Then, use an old paintbrush or vacuum to remove chips and dust from the hole. For deep repairs, apply patching plaster as a base coat. You may need to apply several coats, allowing each to dry to bring the level of the patch even with the rest of the wall. Score each layer of patching plaster to help the next layer bond to it.

2 **Apply the Final Coat.** Apply the final layer of drywall compound or patching plaster using a drywall taping knife. Spread the new material out onto the undamaged area of the wall. After it cures—about 24 hours later—sand smooth, feathering the edges into the surrounding wall.

3 **Prime before Painting.** Prime the repair before painting. The primer helps avoid splotchy areas when the entire wall is painted.

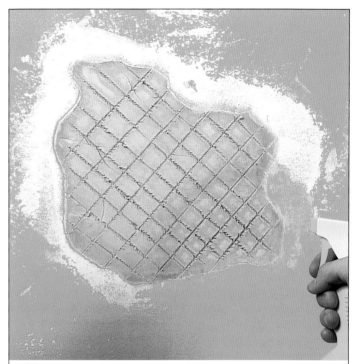

1 Remove the old plaster that is no longer attached to the lath. Undercut the hole with a can opener, giving the new plaster something to grab. Score each coat of plaster; mist the coat before the top coat.

2 Apply the finish coat of plaster using a wide taping knife. The wide knife will help you judge when the repair is even with the surrounding wall.

3 To blend the repair seamlessly with the rest of the wall, you will need to feather the edge of the final coat. Don't be surprised if the patch extends past the original damage. Prime the repair before painting.

Drywall Repair Kits

Drywall surfaces are subject to nicks and dents from a variety of sources. It is not unusual to move a picture or piece of furniture and find a small hole in the drywall where someone hit the wall, left a hole or dent, and then tried to cover the damage. The handle on a swinging door can also damage the wall when there is not a door stop in place. Most of this type of damage will be unnoticeable when repaired and covered with a fresh coat of paint. Check your home center or hardware store for specialized kits that can help you patch damaged drywall.

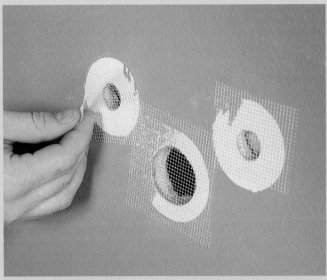

1 Small-hole repair kits come with a self-stick mesh that you simply place over the damage and press to adhere. The mesh gives the patching compound something to grab.

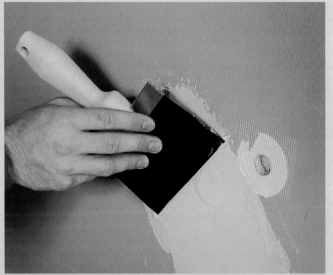

2 Use a putty knife or a drywall taping knife to apply drywall joint compound. Spread the material thinly and feather the edges. Sand smooth, and apply a primer before painting.

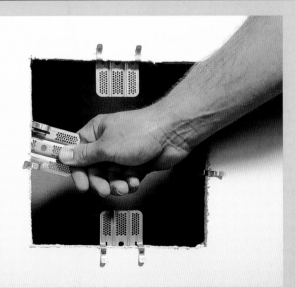

1 For larger holes, use a clip kit. Square off the damaged area so that you can cut a patch from a piece of drywall. Attach the clips as shown.

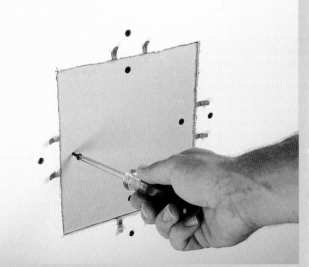

2 Attach the patch with screws. Snap off the clip strips, and cover the entire area with drywall joint compound. Feather the edges so that the patch blends with the surrounding area. Sand smooth; apply a primer.

3 Interior Painting

Patching Larger Holes in Drywall

1 **Delineate the Damaged Area.** Use a framing square to outline the repair area. The object is to make a clean square or rectangle for which you can make a drywall patch. The easiest way to do this is to cut a patch that is larger than the damaged area, and use it as a guide for squaring the area. That way you will have a patch that you know fits.

Drill a hole just inside each of the four corners of the square. Use these holes as starting points for a drywall saw to remove the damaged area. Cut two pieces of 1x4 at least five inches longer than the vertical size of the hole. Hold the 1x4 against the inside vertical edge of the hole exposing half the width. Then secure the 1x4 with a drywall screw above and below the hole. Repeat this procedure on the opposite side. If the patch is larger than about 8 inches, fit horizontal cleats as well.

2 **Install the patch.** Measure and cut a piece of new wallboard to the size of the hole or use the patch you've already created. Secure with construction adhesive and drywall screws driven into the cleats.

3 **Finishing the Edges.** Cover the seams in the patch with perforated drywall tape. Simply press the self-stick tape into place. This will keep the seams of the repair from cracking later. Then apply drywall compound over the tape.

4 **Sand and Prime.** Sand the patch until smooth. Prime the area before painting.

Repairing Corners

Corners are the weak link in drywall surfaces. In many cases, whoever installed the drywall originally simply butted two pieces of drywall together at the corner, taped the joint, and then finished with drywall compound. It does not take much to damage this area, and it is not unusual to find crumbly corners. Even if the contractor did install a metal corner guard—the recommended procedure—damage can still occur. To repair, cut away the damaged area using a utility knife. The goal is to keep from damaging the rest of the wall. If a metal guard is present, use a hacksaw to remove the damaged area. Screw a new piece of guard in place with drywall screws. Finish by applying a coating of drywall joint compound. Feather the edges along the repair. Sand until smooth.

1 Cut away the damaged area. If removing an existing corner guard, cut it using a hacksaw, and pry off of the wall. Attach a new section of corner guard with drywall screws.

2 Apply a coating of drywall joint compound. The corner bead has a slightly raised edge at the joint; use it as a guide for your knife. This will help you apply the compound smoothly.

1 You will need to cut a patch from a spare piece of drywall. Remove the damage, and install 1x4 cleats on each side of the opening. Hold the cleats in place using drywall screws.

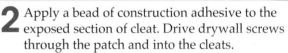

2 Apply a bead of construction adhesive to the exposed section of cleat. Drive drywall screws through the patch and into the cleats.

3 Apply self-stick drywall seam tape to all of the seams in the patch. Simply press the tape in place. Use a putty or drywall knife to apply a coating of drywall joint compound.

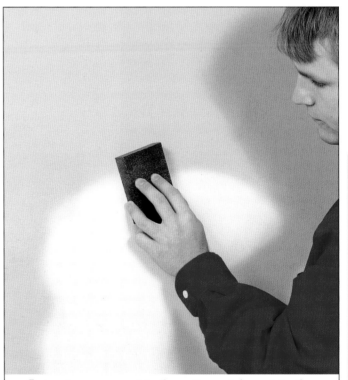

4 Apply compound to the entire patch, and feather the edges for a seamless repair. Sand the area to a smooth finish. Be sure to apply a coat of primer before painting.

Repairing Woodwork

Patch minor nicks and dents in woodwork and trim using wood filler, putty compound, or drywall compound. If yours is a fairly modern house, and replacement wood trim is readily available, it may be easier to replace heavily damaged trim than to patch it. For older houses, especially those with distinctive trim, it is always worth the effort to restore damaged parts. However, oftentimes these types of restorations should be handled by a professional.

1 **Fill the Hole.** Patch nicks and dents with wood filler, spreading the filler with a putty knife or, if necessary, your finger. Fingers are often the best smoothing tool available. Overfill nicks and dents slightly.

2 **Caulk the Gaps.** Caulk is a painter's best friend. Filling the small gaps between trimwork and the wall or where the corners of miter joints have separated is one way of ensuring a professional-quality job. Again, your finger is often the best smoothing tool. (Water keeps the caulk from sticking to your finger.) Use a damp cloth to clean up any stray caulk. Do not try to sand caulk. It will just ball up on sandpaper. To get a sharp edge on a bead of caulk, trim it with a craft knife. Let caulk dry thoroughly before priming or painting the trimwork.

3 **Sand Smooth.** When the filler cures, use 100-grit sandpaper to sand the repair flush with the wood surface.

Stripping Woodwork

Use a cheap acrylic-bristle brush (foam brushes melt). Brushing in one direction, apply as much remover on the work as it will hold. Wait about 5 to 10 minutes, and remove the paint sludge with a putty knife. If the paint sticks to the work piece, wait a few minutes and try again. Usually, some paint remains after one application. Repeat the stripping process until all the paint is removed. If some stubborn spots remain, pick them off with a molding scraper, or sand them off. Some woods, particularly oak, retain paint in tiny depressions within the grain, resisting all efforts of removal.

Wipe down the work piece with clean water, then let it dry thoroughly. At this point, it is ready for sanding and finishing. Interior woodwork also can be stripped using heat guns or heat plates.

1 Apply wood filler using a putty knife or your finger. Work the material into the hole and overfill it slightly. It will shrink as it cures. For new trim pieces, fill all of the nailholes for a pro-quality job.

2 Few materials can neaten up a paint job like a tube of paintable caulk. Apply caulk to all seams where woodwork meets the wall surface. Use it to hide gaps in miter joints as well.

3 Follow the manufacturers directions for drying times of whatever filler you use. When it is dry, sand the patch smooth using a fine-grit sandpaper or a sanding block. The filler should be exactly even with the woodwork.

Removing Wallpaper

It is best to remove old wallpaper before painting a wall. You will be able to strip some papers easily. All you need do is find a seam and begin to peel the paper from the wall. Use warm water to wash off any remaining paste. After this is done, the walls are ready to be primed.

If you cannot simply peel off the wall covering, you will have to scrape it off. You can use a scraper to remove the paper, but scrapers often damage the paper of the drywall underneath the wall covering. This damage must be repaired before painting. A better option is to use a scarifying tool like the one shown here. As you pull the tool along, tiny blades cut through the wallpaper. Sponge or spray the wall with a wallpaper remover or plain water. Give the solution time to soak into the paper; then scrape. Finish up by washing the walls down with plain water.

Wallpaper steamers, available at most tool rental houses, can also remove wallpaper, but they do not speed up the job. Steamers are heavy and difficult to work with, and rental fees are often expensive.

1 Score the Wallpaper. Begin removing the dry wallpaper that easily pulls off by hand. Then use the scarifying tool to create small holes in the surface of the wallpaper. The tool has three legs, each containing tiny blades.

2 Apply the Solution. Use a spray bottle, sponge, or a roller to apply the solution. Wallpaper paste removers are available at home centers and paint stores. The small holes help soak up the solution, so give it time to work. Do not spray more than you can work with in one hour or so. If you do not scrape an area before it dries, your efforts are wasted. Do go back and spray the same area several times before you start scraping. The more times you spray, the better the liquid penetrates, making it easier for you to remove the wallpaper.

3 Remove the Paper. Carefully scrape off all layers of wallpaper and any backing. Do not use so much force that you mar the wall surface. The paper will be wet, so it is best to have a receptacle at hand to hold the paper. A plastic yard bag works well. Wipe down the walls with clean water to remove the last of the paste.

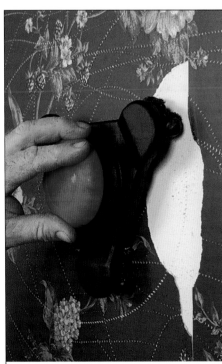

1 To use the score and scrape method of wallpaper removal, run the scoring tool over the surface of the wall. Tiny blades will create small holes in the wallpaper. Run the tool in a random pattern to create the holes.

2 Apply the wallpaper-removal solution. You can use a roller or you can spray the solution on the wall. The important thing is to give the solution time to work its way under the wallpaper.

3 Use a wide putty knife to remove the paper. You may need to reapply the solution for stubborn pieces. When all of the paper is off the wall, wash down the walls with water to remove any leftover residue.

Final Prep & Sanding

When all wall repairs are made and all wall coverings removed, it is time for the final prep and sanding. Wash down walls and woodwork with a household cleaner. This removes any grease or wax that may prevent good adhesion of the paint. Smoke and grease bleed through a new coat of paint, so be sure to prime these areas before painting as part of the final prep work. Set up bright lights to help you work accurately, as well as show defects. Arrange the lights to illuminate the area being worked on and to eliminate shadows.

Cleaning Up. Sanding drywall compound and old paint produces a lot of fine dust that settles on the tops of window, door, and baseboard trim. Some will even cling to walls. Vacuum all surfaces, and wipe them down with a damp cloth. If there is a lot of dust on the drop cloths, take them outside to shake them before putting them back in place.

Masking Hardware & Edges

Some hardware, such as door lock-sets and hinges, should be masked before painting starts. You may also want to protect trimwork, such as window and door casings, baseboards, chair rails, and other trimwork by masking with painter's tape.

Using Painter's Tape. It is best to use painter's masking tape rather than other types because it has a lighter adhesive. It won't stick to the surface when you remove it. It is easier to apply tape in short sections rather than trying to place a long piece. Painter's masking tape is available at paint stores.

Sand repairs, above left, and then wipe down the wall to remove dust. A shopvac is a good cleanup tool. Use a work light to make sure any repairs are smooth and even, above right. Use painter's tape to mask woodwork if desired.

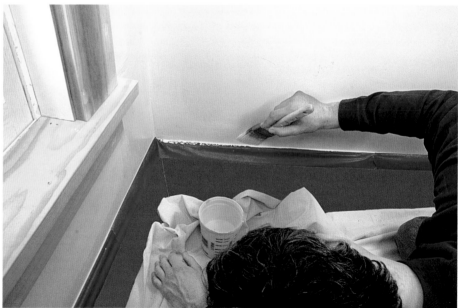

PRO TIP

Having a Rag Ready. Before you start painting, put a dust rag or dust brush in your pocket. This allows you to knock down spiderwebs or to dust the top of a door or window as you work around the room.

Priming

Primer is used to seal in stains and to provide a consistent, slightly grainy surface that enhances the bond between the finish paint and the painted surface. It is also the final, and often most critical, step of interior preparation. Prime all bare and stained wood before painting. Water-stained areas, and those areas that once had wallpaper on them, should be primed with a shellac-based primer.

An added benefit of priming is that it highlights imperfections that otherwise might be missed. This provides a last chance to repair minor defects such as ridges in patches, poorly feathered edges, or nicks and scrapes.

Apply a primer to unpainted drywall and woodwork. Also prime any repairs so that the finished paint job is even throughout.

PRO TIP

Using a Paint Guide. A paint guide helps get paint into tight corners, while keeping it off ceilings or trim. Be careful not to get paint on the back of the paint guide. Clean it often while you work. It is disappointing when a "neatness" tool ends up making a mess.

Picking a Primer

For most priming jobs, any good quality interior primer is sufficient. Most primers are available in water-based (latex acrylic) and oil-based (alkyd) formulas. Oil-based and shellac-based primers do a better job than water-based primers in blocking stains.

Surface to Be Painted	Primer
Unpainted drywall	Drywall primer (It seals the drywall.)
Unpainted woodwork	Oil-based primer
Smoke- and other stained surfaces	Shellac-based primer
Glass, tile, and other slick surfaces	Bonding primer
Gloss or semigloss finish coats	Latex enamel undercoaters
Damp locations, kitchens, and baths	Vapor-barrier primer

Brush Technique

Many people instinctively grab a paintbrush with a handshake grip. A better grip is more like a pencil grip with the fingers and thumb wrapped around or near the metal ferrule. This grip allows the hand and wrist a full range of motion, providing greater precision. If your hand cramps, switch hands or switch temporarily to the handshake grip.

1 **Laying On the Paint.** Dip the brush about 1 inch or so into the paint. Don't cover more than the bottom one-third of the bristles. As you remove the brush from the bucket, tap the brush lightly against the side to remove excess paint. Do not drag the brush across the top of the paint can or bucket. This removes too much paint and creates a mess. The more paint on the brush, the easier the work.

Pulling the brush out of the bucket and across the work surface lays on the paint. The laying-on strokes do not have to be neat. Simply wipe the paint onto the work surface in two strokes, one from one side of the brush, one from the other.

2 **Brushing Out the Paint.** Brush out the paint using long, even, parallel strokes. Use enough pressure to bend the bristles just a little. As you paint, keep a "wet edge." This means painting from a dry area into the previously painted, still-wet area.

3 **Tipping Off the Paint.** Finish off the leading edge of the paint by tipping off, that is, gradually pulling the bristles off the surface. (Think of an airplane leaving the runway and imitate that motion.)

1 Using the right-size brush for the job at hand, dip about 1 in. or so of the bristles into the paint. If painting woodwork, the stroke should flow in the direction of the wood grain.

2 After you have applied paint to the surface, go back and brush out the area. Smooth the paint with the brush.

3 When you come to the edge of the section you are painting, "tip off" the bristles by gradually lifting them from the surface. This helps create a feathered edge. Reload the brush, and paint back to this area.

The Order of Work

There are no rules that say a certain part of the room must be painted first, but in general, rooms are painted from the top down. Begin with the ceiling. If you are priming new drywall, move right from priming the ceiling to priming the walls.

If you are painting the walls a different color than the ceiling, put one coat on the ceiling, let it dry, and then paint the walls. This way you don't need to be fussy about the joint where the wall and ceiling meet when you are painting the ceiling. It is OK to get some ceiling paint on the wall because the wall will be repainted. Just make sure that the ceiling is dry before you tackle the walls. In addition, many people find it easier to cut in a straight line along the top of the wall, as opposed to cutting in along the edge of the ceiling. Of course, cornice molding is a natural divider, so there is no free-form cutting in. If you are adding a second coat, repeat the sequence.

Woodwork. If the woodwork will be a different color than the walls, many people paint the walls, allow them to dry, and then paint the woodwork. In that way, any roller splatters that land on the woodwork will be covered. But many pros paint the woodwork first because the edges of moldings and casings are often extremely narrow, and it is difficult to paint them without getting paint on the

walls. You will need to apply painter's tape and use a paint guide to do a good job. If you paint the woodwork first, you don't need to be concerned about the narrow edge because you can get paint on the walls that will be

covered later. Also, it is easier to cut a clean edge on the vertical wall surface than on the narrow molding. You can always go back later to touch up splatters from the roller.

After priming, paint woodwork using a semigloss paint. This creates contrast between the woodwork and the walls, and it provides a cleanable surface.

Roller Technique

Rollers are much faster than brushes for painting walls and ceilings. Virtually all painters choose to paint walls and ceilings with a roller. Place the cover on the roller. For flat surfaces use a short-nap roller. Textured surfaces require roller covers with longer naps.

1 **Load the Roller.** Dip the roller into the paint and pull it across the ribs on the edge of the pan. Or pull it across the roller screen if you are using a paint bucket.

2 **Apply the Paint.** Apply two strips of paint on the wall. The object here is to get the paint onto the surface. Some people like to apply the paint in a W or M shape.

3 **Smooth the Paint.** Fill in by rolling on the diagonal or horizontal to cover the entire surface. This method helps ensure that there are no gaps in the paint finish. If a bead forms at the edge of the roller, it means you are pressing too hard. Roll on a small section at once. You will get used to how much the roller can hold. Reload the roller, and work back to the area you just painted. Don't place a loaded roller in wet paint on the wall or ceiling. Keep a strong work light trained on the surface to help you spot gaps in the coverage.

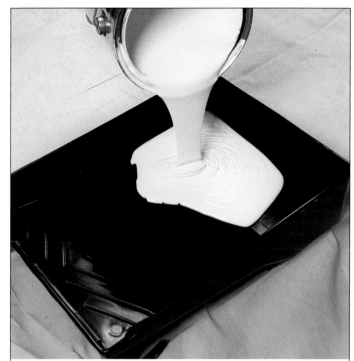

1 Pour the paint into a roller pan or a bucket fitted with a roller screen. Dip the roller in the paint and then drag it across the ribs in the pan to remove excess paint.

2 Apply the paint in two stripes or in a M or W shape. The goal here is to get as much paint on the wall as possible.

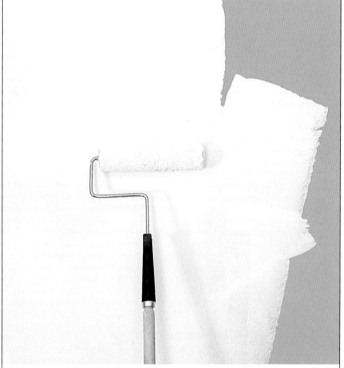

3 Fill in the gaps by rolling horizontally or vertically. Don't apply too much pressure to the roller head because a bead could form where the wall meets the edges of the roller.

Tips for Painting

A new paint job appears splotchy while it is drying. This is normal. Avoid the urge to return to just-painted areas in an attempt to even out the finish. If you are doing a reasonably good job, the finish will look even when it is dry. Let the paint dry thoroughly before judging the color. Other tips:

■ On wood surfaces, such as doors or windows, brush in the direction of the wood grain. All brushing leaves brush marks, but they are less noticeable when they run in the direction of the wood grain.

■ Work from small containers when brushing out paint. Paint stores sell inexpensive plastic or metal buckets that hold a small amount of paint. Keep the lip of the paint can clean by driving a few nails through the lip. That way any paint that accumulates there will drip down into the can. This will make the can easier to open the next time you paint.

■ Check for drips or sags every 10 to 15 minutes as you work. If the paint is still wet, brush out drips or sags. If the paint is tacky, let drips and sags dry completely; then sand out the imperfections and touch up.

■ If you have to stop before the paint job is done, stop at a logical break point such as a corner or the end of a piece to trim. Carry the paint all the way to the break point. Do not worry about getting it on the adjoining unpainted surface. It is better to overrun the break point than to stop short of it.

■ To get a really smooth finish on walls, "knock down" the burrs and raised paint grain by sanding between coats. Take 220-grit sandpaper and lightly go over the walls. This will create a small amount of dust that should be taken off with a damp sponge.

For a smooth finish, sand between coats, above. The results are especially noticeable on woodwork. To keep the lip of the paint can clear, poke a few holes in the lip to allow the paint to drip through, right.

Painting the Ceiling

Rolling a ceiling is no more difficult than rolling the walls. One thing you must be careful about, however, is where you place the paint can. You don't want to knock it over as you study the ceiling above.

1 Cutting in the Ceiling. Use a 2 or 3-inch brush to cut in around the edge of the ceiling. If some paint gets on the wall surfaces, wipe it off with a rag. Cut in around light fixtures and ceiling fans.

2 Checking the Roller. Place the roller cover on the frame, making sure that the end of the cover is flush with the end of the frame. Ceiling work is faster if the roller is mounted on an extension pole.

In this case, place the roller tray on the floor. Some people prefer to work from a ladder to get close-up control of holding the roller handle. In this case, use the hooks on the bottom of the paint tray to secure the tray to the ladder's shelf.

3 Loading the Paint Tray. Fill the bottom portion of the tray with paint. Try to keep the paint off the can label as it is poured, you may need to read the label directions or specifications later. Inexpensive guards (they look like the bill of a cap) keep paint off the label and out of the top of the can. Use a brush to clean up the top of the can, then set the cover loosely on top. Put the can in an out of the way place, preferably just outside the room, so you do not

have to worry about kicking it over as you work.

Dip the roller into the paint. Use the sloped part of the tray to take off the excess. Repeat the process until the roller is saturated but not dripping.

4 Rolling out the Paint. Apply paint in a zigzag "N" or "W" pattern The idea is not to paint neat zigzags (which is hard to do with an extension pole anyway). The idea is to roughly apply the paint, which is spread out evenly. In subsequent strokes lay the zigzag pattern over an area that is within comfortable reach—about 3 feet x 5 feet.

Roll using even strokes that overlap the edges at the beginning and end. Continue painting in sections,

1 Use a small brush to cut in around the edges of the ceiling. This covers areas the roller cannot reach. Here crown molding acts as a natural divider between the wall and ceiling.

2 Attach the roller cover to the frame. For ceilings, consider using an extension handle on the roller. This will save a lot of time and effort climbing up and down ladders.

overlapping from each "new" area into the just-painted area, thus keeping a wet edge. As you come to the end of a stroke, do not simply stop rolling and then lift the roller. Instead, feather it. Watch for roller marks as you apply the paint. Roller marks are thin lines caused by a buildup of paint that flows off the edges of the roller. They are also caused by putting excessive pressure on the roller. If lines appear, try using less pressure. If the paint is not adhering properly, it's probably not because you are pushing too softly. Most likely, it is because the roller needs more paint. Do not make the mistake so many beginners make by "dry rolling." Keep the roller loaded with paint for an even coat.

Check frequently for runs or drips. If you see imperfections in a wet area, eliminate them by going over the area with a fairly dry roller. Be careful not to re-roll areas that have started to become tacky. Doing this causes an "orange peel" effect that may not blend in when the paint dries. If you create an "orange peel" area, sand it out and repaint the entire surface.

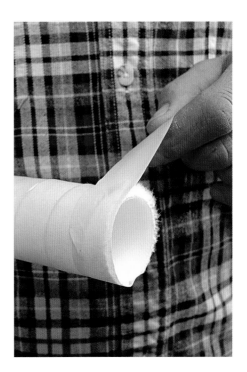

Use masking tape to remove the loose fuzz that sometimes clings to roller covers. Wrap the entire cover with tape, and pull it off. This works for both short- and long-nap covers.

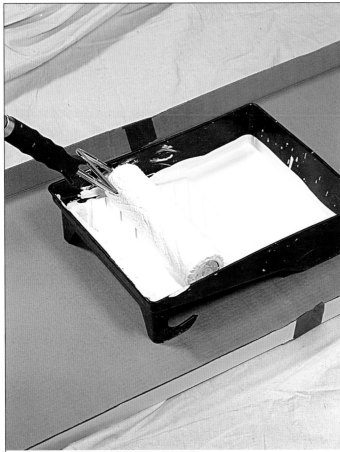

3 Load the roller, and remove excess paint by dragging the roller over the ribs in the pan. To prevent spills, place the pan on a piece of cardboard. A clean, open pizza box is shown here.

4 Work from the edge of the wall back. Start where the light is best so that you can spot skips in the coverage. Work in small sections, and always keep a wet edge.

Painting the Walls

Virtually all jobs require two coats of paint. One exception is a job that requires a color that closely matches the new color. The second coat is applied the same way as the first coat. Avoid the temptation to skip the cutting-in process. Once the paint is dry, this shortcut becomes obvious.

1–2 **Cut In.** Let each ceiling coat dry completely before moving to a wall. Cut in the wall-to-ceiling joint, being careful to draw a straight line at the freshly-painted ceiling. Cut in around doors and windows, in tight areas (less than a roller width) between trim and wall joints, in the corners, and at all wall-to-baseboard joints. (Touch up mistakes at the end of the job.)

If the room is completely cut in and allowed to dry before the rolling begins, a line shows up where the cut-in area meets the rolled area. The effect is very slight, virtually unnoticeable if you are using a high-quality paint. Even with a semigloss paint, this line bothers only the most extreme perfectionists. Keeping a wet edge will prevent the line from appearing. As you cut in along the ceiling, have a helper roll out the area, working along with you.

3–6 **Apply the Paint.** Use the roller technique to apply paint to the walls. Paint two strips and connect them. Or apply paint in a W pattern and fill in. Many pros like to use an extension handle on walls as well as ceilings because it is easier on the shoulders. If using an extension handle, place the roller tray on the floor. If not using an extension handle, place the tray on the paint shelf of a step ladder or on some sort of raised, stable work surface so that you don't need to keep bending to load the roller.

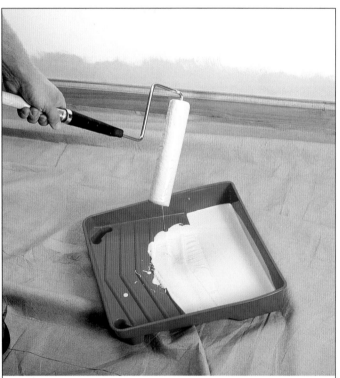

3 Pour the wall paint into a roller tray or a bucket that has a roller screen. Short-nap roller covers are for smooth walls. This information is usually on the roller-cover packaging.

4 Lay on the first strip of paint. The purpose of the first strip is to get the paint onto the walls. Notice the use of a an extension pole for painting walls.

1 Cut in before you start to use the roller. Be sure you will finish the area before stopping for the day. Cut in at the juncture of wall and ceiling, and around any trimwork.

2 You can apply painter's tape to protect the trimwork, but most pros prefer to cut in freehand. It is easier to cut in along the flat surface of the wall.

5 Apply a second strip a short distance from the first. You can also apply the paint in a W-shaped pattern. Just don't make it too large.

6 Connect the painted areas. Use horizontal strokes to fill in the area with paint. Apply light pressure as you move the roller cover across the wall. Tip off the paint by lifting the cover from the surface.

Painting Door & Window Casing

The first decision to make when painting any trimwork is whether to wrap—extend the trim color to all sides of the trim—or face off the casing—paint just the face of the trim. Most modern, post-World War II trim is comprised of flat boards which can be handled either way. In general though, wrapping looks best on thicker moldings. Many older houses have trim with rounded edges that do not provide the sharp edge necessary for facing off. Therefore they must be wrapped. Either way, start at the outside edge of the trim and keep a wet edge as you paint.

Painting Doors

There are two big reasons to paint doors carefully. Because door panels are large, flat surfaces located at eye level, doors get noticed. Secondly, doors are functional moving parts, so you want to avoid a buildup of paint, which prevents doors from closing properly.

Doors should be carefully prepared to remove old paint drips and fat edges and to ensure a good bond between the old and new paint. A good prep job requires sanding. Use a palm sander for the quickest results. If you do not have a palm sander, sand the door by hand. If old runs and drips require coarse sandpaper, start with 60-grit paper

and finish up with 100- or 120-grit paper. You may need to do a little work with a pull scraper to get the door in good functioning order.

For best results, prime doors with a good-quality primer. If the doors are flat, prime the edges with a brush, and then use a roller to prime the faces. Do the same when you apply paint. If the door has raised panels, it should be primed and painted, in this way:

1 Painting Edges. As you paint the edges, use a rag to wipe off paint that accumulates on the front and back of the door.

1 Open the door and paint the latch-side edge. This job will be much neater if you remove the hardware first. If the hinge-side edge will be visible, paint it as well. Keep the door open as the paint dries.

2 For a panel door, paint from the inside out. Start at the panels. Be sure to cover the recess of the panel thoroughly. Brush out any buildup in the bottom corners before the paint dries.

2 Painting Panels. Paint the door panels next, working from the top down.

3 Painting Rails. The rails are the horizontal members at the top, middle and bottom on a two- or four-panel door. Brush out the paint with fine strokes that run the full width of the door.

4 Painting Stiles. The stiles are the vertical members on both sides of the panels. Again, work from top to bottom, and finish with long, continuous brush strokes. Look for drips, sags, and runs as you work. Paint often runs off the corners of the panels. Brush out any imperfections.

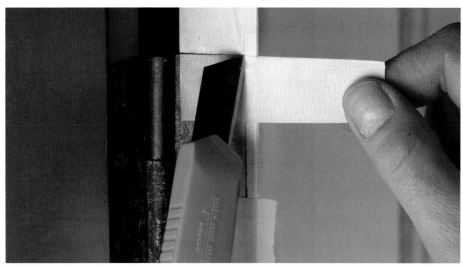

Masking Hinges. If painting the door in place, be sure to mask the hinges. Clean hinges not only look better, they work better, too. Use painter's or masking tape to cover the metal. Cut cleanly using a utility knife rather than trying to tear the tape.

3 Paint the rails next. These are the horizontal members of the door frame. As when painting all woodwork, apply the paint in the direction of the wood grain.

4 Finish up with the vertical stiles of the door. Keep an eye out for paint buildup in the corners and at the bottom of the door. Don't try to brush out tacky paint. Let it dry; remove it; and repaint the area.

Painting Windows

There are three common types of windows: double-hung, casement, and fixed sash. Double-hung windows are the most common; they are the familiar guillotine-type window, with sliding top and bottom sash. Casement windows open like doors—some are controlled by cranks, others are controlled by push rods or handles. Fixed sash windows are those that do not open.

Keeping Paint off Window Parts.

Rule one for painting windows: do not get paint in the window works. Usually this simply means keeping paint out of the window channels. It does not matter if you are painting the windows white and the channels are dark-stained wood. Resist the urge for uniformity. If you paint the channels, the sash will stick and the windows will not work properly. Either live with the contrast in colors, or paint the channels later.

If you are painting older windows that have sash weight cords or chains, do not paint the cords, chains, or pulleys. If you get paint on these parts, there is a good chance that the windows will not work properly. With casement windows, be sure to keep paint out of the cranks, push rods, handles, and hinges.

Freeing a Stuck Window.

If you find that a window sash was painted shut during the last paint job, free it by using a putty knife or utility knife to cut the paint film binding the sash to the window frame. The window may be painted shut on the inside or outside. Do not bang on the window sash with a hammer. If a window needs a little "persuading," place a wood block against the sash and tap gently. Be careful not to knock sash corners apart.

Double-Hung Windows

If you have not already removed the sash lock hardware, do it now. Place the hardware in plastic bags so small parts and screws do not get lost. Apply only one coat of paint to meeting edges such as sash rails and sash-to-frame joints. A paint buildup at these joints can prevent the window from opening and closing easily

When you paint the window sash, it is nearly impossible to keep paint off the glass. Fortunately, dried paint comes off glass very easily, so when painting the sash, let the paint lap onto the glass about $\frac{1}{8}$ to $\frac{1}{4}$ inch. After the paint dries, remove the overlap with a razor blade.

1 Pull the upper sash down an inch or so, and paint the top rail, the sides, and any muntins present. Paint as much of the top sash as you can reach. About ⅛ in. of paint should flow onto the glass.

2 Push the top sash down and the bottom sash all the way up. Complete the parts of the top sash that you were not able to reach. With the palms of your hands push the top sash up, but not all of the way.

1 Beginning the Upper Sash. Pull the upper sash down at least an inch to make it easier to paint the top rail. Check the top edge of each sash for any paint buildup. Sand or scrape off fat edges (if any). Paint buildup on the top of either sash can prevent the window from closing properly.

2 Finishing the Upper Sash. Push the lower sash all the way up. Then pull the upper sash down to expose the unpainted bottom portion. Finish painting the upper sash. Push the upper sash up to within about an inch of closing to let the top rail dry before pushing it into its channel.

3 Painting the Lower Sash. Pull the lower sash down to a comfortable level for painting. Do not push it into the bottom channel. This allows you to paint the entire bottom rail. Paint the lower sash working from top to bottom.

4 Removing Paint from Glass. Use a straightedge to score a line along the glass where the paint will end. Then use a window scraper to remove the paint. This tool is designed to hold a single-edged razor blade. You can also use a razor blade to remove the paint.

Casement Windows. Casement windows are painted in this order: hinge edge; muntins; top, bottom, and sides of sash; and finally the frame. Remember to sand out fat edges before painting. Keep paint out of hinges. When the paint becomes tacky, rotate the sash in and out slightly to break the paint film.

Flashing. Flashing is a shiny spotting effect that occurs when wet paint is applied over an area of dry paint. The painted area may flash even if you use the same paint, from the same can, applied with the same brush within a half-hour. High-gloss paints are more prone to flashing than semigloss or flat paints, and some colors tend to flash more than others. Keeping a wet edge helps prevent flashing.

Flashing is not much of a consideration for most inferior painting jobs that use low-gloss latex paint. However, if semigloss or gloss paint is used, you must be careful about keeping a wet edge. Flashing is obvious on touch-ups on enamel painted wood trim, such as doors and window frames.

If the paint flashes, there is no way to fix it. Either live with the results or do the job over carefully, while keeping a wet edge.

3 Here's how the sashes should be positioned while the paint is still wet. Paint the bottom sash. As the paint dries, periodically move the sashes up and down in their channels to keep the paint from sticking.

4 Use a straight-edge razor to remove the dried paint from the glass. There are masking tapes and even liquids available to keep paint off the glass, but the razor approach works well.

Pausing & Stopping

If you must pause or stop in the middle of the job, do not simply drop everything and run. There are a few things that need to be done first.

Pausing a Brush Job. It you need to pause a brush job for an hour or two, wrap the brush in plastic wrap and place it out of sunlight. The plastic wrap keeps the paint from drying out. Close the paint can and place it out of sunlight as well. To put the job on hold overnight, wrap the brush thoroughly in plastic wrap, and store it in the refrigerator. Cooling the brush delays evaporation for several hours. A brush can be stored overnight or longer by soaking it in water or turpentine, depending on the base of the paint being used.

Pausing a Roller Job. To pause for an hour or two, dip the roller to thoroughly load it, but do not roll out the excess. Cover the tray with a piece of plastic wrap. To stop overnight, double-wrap the fully-loaded roller in plastic wrap and store it in the refrigerator.

You can clean nylon roller covers, but it takes a long time to wash all the paint out of them, and most people consider them cheap enough to discard at the end of the job. That said, a good lamb's wool roller is worth the effort of a thorough washing. Store the roller on end or by hanging it, so it does not develop a flat spot. Clean the roller frame and paint tray outside if possible. If necessary, finish cleaning over a sink, using warm water and a small amount of dish-washing liquid. Rinse out the sink drain thoroughly. If you are rolling oil-based paint, it is never worth cleaning a nylon roller cover. Clean a good-quality lamb's wool roller by soaking it thoroughly in turpentine and mineral spirits three times.

Cleaning Up

Even when the paint job is finished, there is a lot of work left to be done. Besides cleaning off yourself, you will want to clean all of your tools so they remain in good condition.

Latex. Use small amount of dish-washing liquid and plenty of running water to remove latex from yourself and your painting tools. Squeeze the brush frequently, and use a wire brush to get paint out of the area around the ferrule. If you are working in a sink or bathtub, let the water run for a few minutes after you have cleaned everything to make sure the paint clears out of the drain. Gummed up paint clogs plumbing. Shake the brush out then slap it across a clean, dry surface to remove the last of the water. Place the brush back in its protective jacket (or a piece of butcher paper) and hang it on a hook.

Oil-Based. Wear rubber gloves to protect your hands. Wash the brush repeatedly in an inch or two of mineral spirits, squeezing and massaging the brush frequently to remove built-up paint. Clean the ferrule area gently with a wire brush. When you think the brush is clean (mineral spirits coming out of the brush run clear), do one final rinse in a clean container of mineral spirits. Shake and slap the brush dry. Then store it in a protective jacket or butcher paper.

Removing Drips. After the painting is done and the drop cloths are removed, you may find a paint drip or two. If it is oil-based paint, let it dry thoroughly, then try to pop it off the surface with a razor blade. If the drip is on carpet, "shave" it off with a razor blade. If the drip is latex paint, buff it with a damp cloth, if that does not work, wipe it up with a commercial paint remover.

Discarding the Leftovers. What to do with leftover paints and solvents, such as mineral spirits and paint thinner, is an environmental issue that has yet to be resolved. Many waste disposal contractors will not knowingly pick up or discard paint, paint cans, or solvents. To determine the rules and requirements in your town, call the local waste-disposal agency (or contractor). Local practices vary. In some areas, you can empty latex paint into old newspaper or kitty litter, and let the remnants in the can dry. Dispose of them in the trash. Oil-based paint cannot be placed in the trash. (For more on cleaning tools and disposing of paint, see Chapter 6, page 100.)

Spinning the brush clean, right, is a great way to clean the brush without damaging it. Spin inside a 5-gallon bucket for the best results.

The easiest way to avoid having leftover paint that must be discarded is to take great care when estimating your required quantity. It's easy to buy more paint than you need to save yourself the trip to the paint store, but it does tax the waste stream—and potentially compromise air quality, indoors and out—to have lots of extra paint lying around.

Clean up after using oil-based paint, opposite, involves using paint thinner or turpentine. Wear rubber gloves for protection.

Rinse brushes used with water-based paint, left, under running water. A brush comb helps remove paint from the bristles.

Decorative Paint Finishes

Take your skills one step further with the techniques described below to create decorative finishes. These techniques are surprisingly simple to learn. Yet you can use them to create faux finishes that can turn an ordinary room into a unique place that expresses your own creativity.

For a decorative finish to look good, start with a well-prepared surface and a good base coat of solid color. Cover floors and any furniture in the room with drop cloths. Repair walls if necessary.

Glazing Techniques

Decorative paint techniques all employ the same formula of a base color that shows through the broken color and translucence of one or more top coats of colored glaze. The differences lie in whether the glaze is added or subtracted on the surface and how it is moved about. Results are quite pleasing with simple rags moved skillfully, but can be even more striking by using special brushes and tools. One of the keys to decorative finishes is to have a consistent flow, even in broken color effects. Keep your hand moving. Don't go back over an area until the project is dry, and then add color sparingly. Use a special glaze for the top coat or even thinned latex paint.

Sponging. Use the sponging technique for walls, ceilings, flat-surfaced furniture, and cabinets. Sponging creates an illusion of depth by having multiple layers of broken color over a base color. This is perhaps the easiest of all the techniques, as the goal is a random, uneven pattern. Simply load the sponge with glaze and dab. Don't over-sponge or you'll get muddled and splotchy areas instead of the fields of dotted color you are after. It is best to use a natural sea sponge because of the irregular shape, but a synthetic sponge can be torn to remove all flat surfaces and edges. Sponging looks best with multiple layers of color over the base. For subtle depth, use varying shades of one color over the base.

Ragging. Ragging is for walls, doors, and flat-surfaced furniture. The success of this finish depends on the colors in your glaze, the contrast to the base coat, and primarily upon what type of material is used to add or subtract one or more coats of glaze. A rule of thumb is that the less porous the material used, the more striking the pattern created. The most common material (for an elegant and mellow effect) is soft, clean, lint-free cotton squares. Cut these squares from old clothing or bedding but watch for loose threads. Cheesecloth also makes a soft pattern. More striking surfaces are made with pliable, lint-free materials, such as lace, canvas, or burlap.

Stippling. Stippling works well for any surface, even curved molding. This finish is similar to sponging, but is much more refined, as the glaze is simply moved

Sponging

Ragging

and transformed with a finely bristled stippling brush. Stippling is more difficult than any rag technique because imperfections will show. Rag application is inherently varied but stippling makes a delicate, slightly elevated, consistent finish. The technique absolutely needs a smooth, well-prepared surface. The base coat should be an oil-based gloss, and the glaze must be oil to maintain workability.

Splattering. This method showers the base coat with tiny droplets of paint or glaze. One way to deliver the paint is to load an oval sash brush and then tap the ferrule of the brush against a stick or another brush handle. The technique can create a deep, textured surface that is alive with color. Try to load the brush with the same amount of paint each time. This will help you achieve an even distribution of color.

Combing. This technique is similar to dragging except it creates a visually more interesting pattern. The dragging brush creates stripes that are gently blended together, whereas combing makes more distinct lines. By using different tools, some which you can make yourself, patterns are created where the glaze is lifted off. As with all of the techniques, move your hand steadily to a stopping point. If you muddle an area or stop midpoint, the surface must be reglazed and started over. Colors can be vivid to highlight patter or similar to suggest patterns.

Stippling

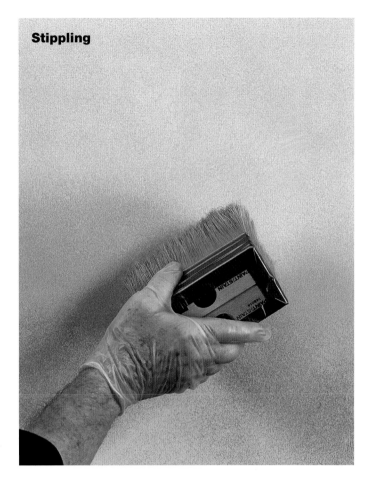

Splattering

Combing

exterior painting

Surface Preparation

The quality of a paint job can be no better than the quality of the prep work. Before you apply paint or primer, you must clean the surface, remove loose paint, and repair any damaged areas. This will provide a clean, smooth surface that will bond with the paint.

For a previously painted house, look closely at how the old paint job fared over the years. If there are problems, the solution usually calls for fixing whatever caused the problem and scraping the damaged area down to bare wood. But doing a little detective work now may prevent you from making the same mistake again when you repaint. Here are some conditions you may encounter.

Peeling

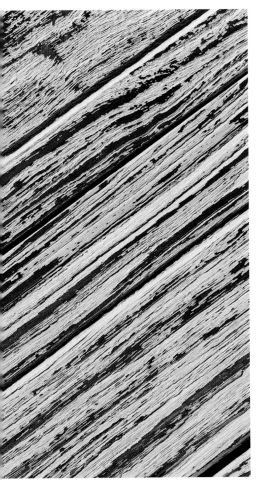

Peeling Paint. Paint usually peels because something is making the wood behind the paint wet. The wet wood swells and helps to break the bond of the film of paint. Often, peeling paint can be attributed to interior moisture vapor making its way through the walls of the house. Leaks inside the wall due to a leaky gutter or ice dams can also cause paint to peel. Another possible cause is paint that was applied to a dirty or oily surface.

Older houses with many coats of paint sometimes peel after receiving a fresh coat of paint. If paint layers have built up to a "critical mass," an extra coat is often enough to break the weak bond between the paint and the wood underneath.

Fix the problem before repainting. For interior moisture problems, make sure that kitchen and bathroom ventilation fans are working properly and that all wall vapor barriers are in place. Scrape all loose paint down to bare wood. When there is a large area that is peeling, pros prefer to remove all old paint down to wood.

Blistering Paint. Blistering paint looks as though it has bubbled up from the surface of the wall, as opposed to peeling off in sheets. In these cases, the paint could have been applied over a damp, oily, or dirty surface. Or water vapor may be migrating out of the interior of the house—often the case around kitchens, bathrooms, and laundry rooms. You can diagnose the problem by cutting into a blister. If you find raw wood, interior moisture is the culprit; if you find paint still attached to the surface of the wall, the last person who painted the house did so over a damp or dirty surface.

Alligatoring. Alligatored paint, true to its name, looks like alligator skin—you'll know it when you see it. Applying paint in thick coats can cause this problem. Working on a hot day in direct sunlight can make the paint dry too quickly, another possible cause. Sometimes multiple paint jobs lead to alligatoring because the buildup of paint over the years simply fails. Using a top coat that is incompatible with whatever is under it can also lead to alligatoring.

Chalking. When paint film starts to break down, it decomposes into a layer of fine dust. Run your hand over the paint. If you pick up a layer of light-colored dust, the paint is chalking. Before primer or paint is applied, the residue must be scrubbed with trisodium phosphate (TSP), followed by a thorough pressure-washing.

Alligatoring

Chalking

Removing Old Paint

There are many ways to "skin" the house. Peeling and cracking paint must be removed before primer and new paint are applied.

Scraping Paint

Scraping is the low-tech way to remove paint; it is also the least toxic method to use. While labor intensive, it is a fairly simple and tidy method to remove paint.

The best tool for the job is a pull scraper, which is a two-hand tool that consists of a long handle and a big knob over the blade end. The blades dull quickly, so keep plenty on hand, and change them often. When using a pull scraper, keep the blade flat on the surface. If you rotate the scraper, the edge of the blade digs in and scars the wood.

Because you cannot always exert as much downward pressure on push scrapers—the tools that have flat blades and look like putty knives—they tend to remove less paint. However, they are handy when using a heat gun because they require only one hand. You can run the heat gun just ahead of the scraper, which easily lifts the softened paint. (See "Stripping Paint with Heat," page 79.) It might be good to have one on hand just to give your pulling muscles an occasional break. One advantage of using push scrapers is that they send the chips flying away from you.

If your house has highly detailed molding such as dental or egg-and-dart trim, or highly ornate window and door casings, you will likely need molding scrapers. Molding scrapers come in shapes that match common molding profiles and usually are available at home centers.

Remove flaking paint using a pull scraper. The knob over the blade gives you enough leverage to sheer the paint film away from the wood. Scrape until you reach sound paint.

Safety First

The following is a list of the basic safety tools you will need for a scraping or sanding job:

■ A pair of **heavy gloves** and a **long-sleeved shirt.** If the blade slips, your hands and arms are protected.

■ A **dust mask,** preferably an N95 mask that catches fine particles. A paper mask rated for nuisance dust is often sufficient. However, houses painted before the mid-1970s are likely to have some lead-based paint. If you have much scraping to do on an older home, use a **respirator** rated for lead dust. If you wear a respirator, bear in mind that the act of breathing, and the work itself, will take more effort. If you have heart or respiratory problems, check with your physician before exerting yourself while wearing a respirator.

■ **Eye protection.** Wear safety glasses, or better yet, goggles. Goggles afford better eye protection, but they also tend to fog up.

Sanding Old Paint

If your house suffers from large areas of peeling, alligatored, or blistered paint, or if there are many layers of paint to remove, sanding may be the best option. Sanding is the quickest way to get shingles or clapboards down to bare wood. Do not try to do the job with a sanding attachment for your power drill. You need a rotary disk sander, sometimes called a disk grinder. This is a heavy duty machine that takes two hands to operate. Use paper or fiber-backed sanding disks. You can buy the sander and disks at paint and home center stores.

Sanding is quick and effective, but it is hard, messy work. Dust is the biggest problem, so you need to put down drop cloths and clean up the site at the end of the work day. Nonetheless, dust still swirls and blows around in the wind. Some sanders come with collection bags, but if you use one of these, be wary of striking a nailhead, creating a spark, and in turn, causing a flash fire.

Lead Alert. Even though you will be working outdoors, lead paint can still pose a hazard. Follow the personal protection advice in "Safety First," above, but also keep children and pregnant women away from the work site as much as possible.

For spot sanding, use a sanding block or section of sandpaper wrapped around a wood block. The support will allow you to exert more pressure on the damaged area and remove more material. You will need to spot sand any minor repairs.

Sanding Tips. Most jobs need to be sanded twice. Use 16-grit disks for aggressive paint removal. Then give the surfaces a quick, light pass with 60-grit sandpaper to smooth it enough for painting. If you want a finer finish, move to a high-grit paper. Powerful sanders sometimes leave permanent marks on the surface. Keep the sander moving and do not dwell on one area, or the sander will dig into the wood and create a recessed, semicircular pattern that the paint highlights. Resist the temptation to turn the sander at an angle. This seems to take paint off faster, but in fact creates gouges in the wood. Keep the sanding disk parallel with the surface at all times.

Order of Work. Start by closing all windows near the work area. Lay drop cloths or sheet plastic to catch the chips, and be sure that all power cords are untangled.

1 Sanding Clapboard. Turn the sander on, lower the disk carefully onto the siding, and turn it up only after you see how the sandpaper is cutting. Keep the sander moving horizontally, while you apply light, constant pressure. Sand as much as you can comfortably reach into both sides until bare wood is exposed.

Once the wood on top is bare, move down without stopping or turning the disk at an angle. Work left and right, as far as you can comfortably reach.

2 Sanding the Edges. Next, sand the bottom edge of the clapboards or siding. Do this by turning the sander at a 90-degree angle to the siding. Use a very light touch. You are sanding a very small surface

with a lot of sander, and you can chew off a noticeable chunk of siding before you realize it.

3 Scraping the Corners. The sanding disk will not reach into corners where siding meets vertical trim. In most cases, the easiest way to remove this paint is with a molding scraper.

1 To remove large areas of paint or to sand the entire house, use a disk sander. Hold the sanding head against the wood, and work in the direction of the wood grain.

2 To remove paint from the exposed edges of clapboards, turn the head 90 deg. to place the sanding head on the edge of the clapboard. Apply light pressure in this area.

3 The disk sander won't be able to reach into corners or where two building components butt together. For these areas, use a molding scraper or a small pull scraper.

Stripping Paint

Stripping paint is usually accomplished using heat or a chemical stripper that is brushed onto the wood. The good thing about stripping is that it removes paint down to the original surface. After painting, the stripped wood can look like new again. However, there are some potentially bad consequences of stripping paint.

It is messy, time-consuming, labor-intensive work, and the most effective chemical paint strippers are toxic. Stripping a door or molding that lost its detail to built-up paint is one thing, but stripping a whole house is something much more ambitious. If the scope of the whole job appears to be overwhelming, consider hiring a professional. Painting contractors use proprietary chemical stripping methods to strip an entire house.

To decide on a paint-stripping contractor, ask for and check the company's references. If your house is very old, check with local historical societies to recommend companies that specialize in stripping old buildings.

Stripping Paint with Heat. For most exterior stripping projects, heat stripping is the way to go. Years ago, painters used blowtorches to strip houses. They simply turned the torch on the paint until it bubbled, and then they scraped it off.

Obviously, there were problems with this approach, and more than a few houses burned to the ground. Blowtorches easily ignite wood and hidden debris such as a bird's nest. In addition, the heat from a blowtorch volatilizes lead in lead-based paint, producing a toxic gas. Do not strip paint with a blowtorch, and do not let anybody else do it on your house.

These days, there are two good tools for heat stripping: the heat gun and the heat plate. Heat guns are best for uneven surfaces, such as trim and molding. Heat plates make fast work of flat surfaces, such as siding. These tools generate enough heat to set wood or hidden debris afire, but they pose much less risk than using a blowtorch.

Use a push scraper for most heat stripping. When stripping paint from molding, use a molding scraper that conforms to the profile of the molding. (These are available at most paint and hardware stores.) Ingenious practitioners have gone so far as to use old spoons and dental picks as molding scrapers.

Using a Heat Gun. Heat guns are essentially industrial-strength blow dryers. They vary widely in quality. Most inexpensive heat guns cannot be repaired. When the heating element or blower motor burns out or breaks, the gun is useless. Professional-quality guns are worth the price if you have a lot of wood to strip.

Heat guns can remove old paint quickly and effectively. They work especially well on flat surfaces, such as the trimwork shown here. Heat the paint; when it bubbles, remove with a scraper or putty knife.

Although heat guns generally do not heat paint to a high enough temperature to volatilize lead, it can happen, so wear a mask or respirator rated for toxic fumes. Using a heat gun is fairly straightforward. Hold the gun a few inches away from the paint you want to strip, and move the gun over a small area. When the paint bubbles, scrape it off with a push scraper. Keep the gun moving. Be careful not to ignite the paint or scorch the underlying wood. If you do scorch the wood, sand it down until you come to good wood.

Be careful not to direct the hot air from the heat gun into any openings in the house. Small openings are often home to wasps and birds, both of which make flammable nests. Keep a fire extinguisher handy as you work, and stay at the job site for an hour or so after you finish to ensure that no smoldering fires catch.

PRO TIP

A heat gun does not remove paint from brick or metal. These materials simply absorb the heat, and have to be chemically stripped. Heat stripping is for wood. If you have vinyl siding on your house, keep the heat gun away from it. A heat gun melts vinyl siding.

Once the chips of paint cool off, sweep them up. Remember, they might contain lead, so check with local waste disposal authorities for rules and regulations on their disposal.

Using a Heat Plate. A heat plate is essentially a heating element with a metal cover over it attached to a handle. Hold the heat plate an inch or two above the paint. Wait until the paint bubbles, and then scrape it off. As with the heat gun, be careful not to ignite the paint or scorch the underlying wood.

Using Chemical Strippers. Chemical stripping of a large area is a big, messy, expensive job. For the best combination of stripping and safety, use a paste stripper that contains methylene chloride.

Caution: Methylene chloride is a "potential occupational carcinogen," according to OSHA, so wear a mask rated for toxic fumes. Less expensive, and less effective, strippers are strongly alkaline and can cause nasty burns. Eye protection is a must when using chemical strippers—they can literally blind a person. Wear an old long-sleeve shirt and heavy gloves with the understanding that the clothing and gloves will be thrown away when the job is done.

For chemical stripping, be sure to use a thick gel-like product that will stick to vertical surfaces. Remove paint using a putty knife. Have a box handy to hold scraped-off paint, rather than letting it fall to the ground.

1 These steps show how paint stripper works inside and outside. For vertical surfaces, such as the trimwork on a house, use a thick, paste-like stripper that will not drip off of the wood.

Strippers advertised as "safe" are still powerful stuff. While less toxic than the methylene chloride strippers, they take longer to work. There are proprietary whole-house chemical stripping systems that are available to specialized contractors. The most common one has stripper embedded in a sort of plastic-covered solution, which is applied over the area to be stripped. When the solution comes off, so does the paint (most of it anyway). This kind of job is neat compared to a do-it-yourself job. Consider hiring a contractor who does this type of work.

Each stripper is formulated differently, so follow the directions on the container. A few rules apply to almost all chemical strippers. They do not work in cold weather, so the hotter the weather the better. Do not consider chemical stripping until the weather reaches the mid-70s. Most strippers must be neutralized either

with water or alcohol before the surface accepts paint again. Read the container directions carefully.

Regardless of the type of chemical stripper, the job involves using a disposable brush to apply stripper liberally waiting a few minutes for the stripper to work, then scraping off the paint. Depending on the quality of the stripper, the temperature, and the dwell time (elapsed time of stripper on the surface), the process might have to be repeated.

Here are some step-by-step guidelines.

1 Laying on the Stripper. Using an old brush (do not use a foam brush, it will melt), liberally apply chemical stripper. Do not brush out the stripper as you would paint. Just lay it on roughly, and leave it.

It is important to give the stripper time to work and make all the paint bubble away from the surface. This usually takes about 10 minutes.

2 Removing the Paint. Using a push scraper, remove the paint from the surface. Use coarse steel wool to remove stripper from curved areas such as moldings. Repeat earlier steps, as necessary.

3 Neutralizing the Stripper. Wipe down the stripped surface with clean water, or with alcohol as specified on the container.

2 Give the stripper enough time to loosen the paint. The directions on the container will specify time periods. When time is up, remove with a flat-blade knife.

3 You may need to apply a second coating of stripper for stubborn areas. Wipe down the wood with clean water or alcohol. Check the container for specific directions.

Repairing Damaged Wood

Damaged wood is always repaired as part of the prep work. No paint job looks good applied over damaged wood, and if the wood is water-damaged, the paint most likely will not adhere to the surface.

Before repairing water-damaged wood, be sure to locate the source of the water and eliminate it. Leaky gutters and downspouts are frequent offenders. Some wood pieces, such as modern windowsills and some moldings, are available in stock sizes. Stock materials often can be replaced more easily than they can be repaired.

Damaged wood can be repaired in place by patching. Many exterior-patching products are available, including exterior spackling and wood putty. The best materials for exterior patching, although a bit on the expensive side, are two-part epoxies. Even severely damaged wood can be repaired this way. These proprietary, two-step systems consist of a thin liquid that is poured onto damaged wood to harden it, followed by a patch made of two-part epoxy. In some cases, two components are mixed together and then applied to the damaged wood, forming a patch when it cures. Epoxy patches can be sanded, drilled, and worked with power tools. Generally, the epoxy patch is stronger than the surrounding wood. Prime and paint epoxy patches as you would with wood.

If you have ornate, or unique features such as old moldings, window and door surrounds, or column bases, have them repaired by a good carpenter.

Begin the patching job by removing as much damaged wood as possible. Try to give the patch a firm base to grab and hold.

1 Mixing the Epoxy. Thoroughly mix the parts according to manufacturer's instructions. Typically it's one part resin to one part hardener. Mix on a board, not in a container. Epoxy works by a heat reaction. If you mix too much of it in a small container, the heat may build up to a point where it ruins the epoxy before you get a chance to use It.

2 Applying the Epoxy. Using a putty knife, apply the epoxy patching material. Work quickly. Once the epoxy starts to harden, you will not be able to spread it. Use a putty knife to work the epoxy into shape to match the damaged piece. When the epoxy starts to harden, stop working.

3 Shaping the Patch. When the epoxy is cured, sand it into shape. You can also shape it quite successfully with a wood chisel.

1 Epoxy wood repair products usually consist of two elements that are combined to form the patch material. These are potent products, so do the mixing outside on the work site.

2 Remove as much damaged wood as possible. For best results, apply to a clean, dry surface. Work the epoxy into the wood.

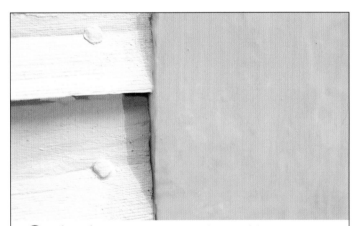

3 When the epoxy is dry, sand or mold it into the shape you want. Molding works well when repairing the rounded area of a stair tread. Cover with a primer, and paint for a seamless repair.

Caulking

Caulking is an essential part of the prep work for an exterior paint job. Besides preventing air leaks around windows, doors, and construction joints, caulk keeps water out. Caulk is also known as "carpenter's helper" because it fills in cracks and gives a seamless appearance to woodwork. "A little caulk and a little paint makes a carpenter what he ain't."

Silicone caulk is expensive, but gives the best performance. A high-quality silicone caulk withstands temperature and humidity changes better than other types. The one disadvantage to using silicone caulk is that it cannot be painted. Hence, it is best to save silicone for joints that are not readily visible. For joints that are to be painted, the best choices are latex and acrylic caulks.

PRO TIP

If you don't use a full tube of caulk and you want to store it, insert a framing nail into the tip. The caulk will dry around the nail, but when the nail is removed, it will open a clear passage to the wet caulk.

A neat bead of caulk can hide a multitude of flaws. No self-respecting painting contractor would be without an ample supply of paintable caulk to complete the prep work on a house. Use caulk to provide a tight seal where two building components meet, such as where clapboard meets a corner board or window casing. Check the corners of window casing, and use caulk to hide any gaps in the miter cuts.

Repairing Windows

Before repainting, closely inspect the windows for loose glazing putty. If you find any, it will have to be removed and replaced.

1 Removing Loose Putty. Use a molding scraper to scrape out the old putty. Stubborn putty can be removed by heating it. Use an electric soldering iron applied directly to the putty. (Do not use a heat gun—the blast of hot air can cause window glass to break.)

Do not obsess over removing the last dregs of putty. If it is stuck tight, it does not need to come off. If the scraper does not move, it might be caught on a glazing point, which are little metal triangles pushed into the sides of the muntins to help hold the glass in place.

2 Cleaning the Surface. Brush out pieces of dust and dirt from the window channel to provide a clean surface. Replace glass and secure with glazing points.

3 Placing the Putty. Replace damaged putty with new glazing putty. Pull the putty out of the can with your hand and roll it into a cylinder that is roughly the diameter of a pencil. If the putty sticks to your hands, put a little linseed oil on your hand before working it. If the putty crumbles, it has dried out and you need to get fresh material. Place the putty on the windows, squeezing it against the muntins and the glass.

1 Repair damaged windows or cracking and crumbling glazing putty before painting. Remove the glass and scrape out the old putty. Note: Always wear heavy gloves when working with glass.

2 Brush out the old putty to get the surface as clean as possible. Use an old paintbrush or a shopvac. Press glazer's points into the window channels.

4 Shaping the Putty. Dip a putty knife in linseed oil to prevent sticking. Place the knife at a 45-degree angle to the window glass; then pull the knife across in one stroke to form a seal. You may need to practice this a few times, but once you get the hang of it, the putty will look as though it has always been there. This is a warm-weather job; cold glazing putty does not form. You'll need to prime the putty before painting. Check the container for curing times.

Dealing with Wasps and Bees

Bees build hives in exterior walls. Bees are usually fairly obvious—you can see them coming and going through a hole in the house. Don't try to fight bees. Call a professional.

A careful prepainting inspection of the house may reveal wasp nests under the eaves. Wipe out nests using long-range wasp and hornet spray. This is one of those cases where using poison is preferable to running into wasps at the top of an extension ladder.

The most dangerous wasps are those hidden behind soffit or fascia boards. Wasps find tiny holes in them, and build nests in the attic. Use an extension pole to tap along the area where you are working. If wasps appear, call a professional.

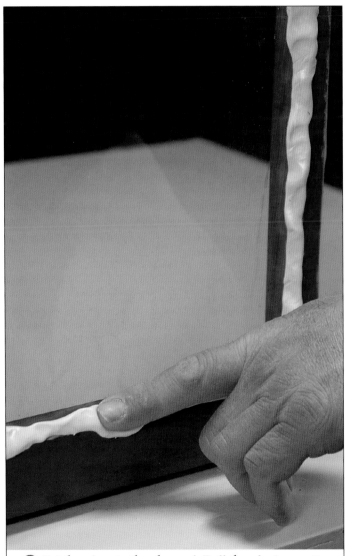

3 Set the glass in the channel. Roll the glazing putty into a long rope to fit into the window channels. Place the rope over the channel, and press it into place. Do all of the channels at once.

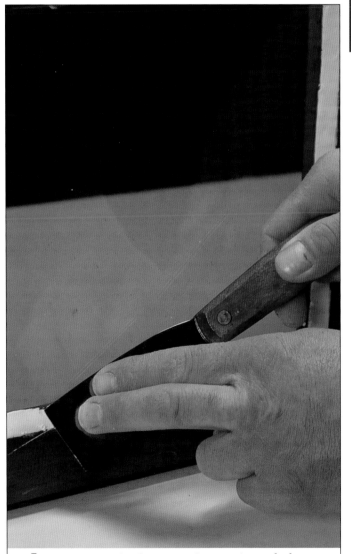

4 Hold a putty knife at a 45-deg. angle, with the knife resting against the edge of the window frame. Pull the knife from one end of the channel to the other. Allow the putty to cure before painting.

Priming

Before the house is primed or repainted, it must be thoroughly cleaned to remove dirt, grease, and chalking. As noted earlier, a professional house washing contractor is often the easiest and best way to go. If you do it yourself, the simplest and best way is by washing it by hand. Use a solution of trisodium phosphate (TSP), available at paint stores. Put on rubber gloves and goggles. With a scrub brush attached to a pole, wash down the exterior surfaces. Rinse the house with a garden hose and then rinse off plants below to keep them from being burned by the TSP solution.

This job is done more quickly with a pressure washer, which is available at most rental supply houses. However, these tools can be troublesome and even dangerous. They can blow out mortar, drive water into and through walls, and propel a person off a ladder. If you want to have your house pressure washed, hire a professional who has insurance. If you want to do the job yourself, stick to hand washing.

Exterior Primers & Sealers

Priming is not so much the first coat of paint as it is the last step of preparation. Primer allows the finish paint to stick—and stay stuck—to the painted surface. Primer also keeps stains, such as turpentine that weeps out of knots in wood, from bleeding through the finish coats. Match primer to the material to be painted. A good wood primer is not necessarily a good metal primer. To make sure you get the right primer, ask for advice at a paint store. Make sure you read the directions and specifications on the label.

Wood Primers. Exterior wood, plywood, or hardboard must be primed with latex or oil-based wood primer. As with finish paint, latex primers can be cleaned up with soap and water, while oil-based primers must be cleaned up with solvents such as mineral spirits.

Oil-based primer has a moderate advantage in its ability to hold out stains, such as the turpentine that weeps from knots in wood. However, oil primer tends to pop off wet wood. If water gets between the wood and the primer (one common source is vapor drive—water vapor that migrates out from the house), oil primer loses its bond, causing the paint to peel down to the bare wood. Most pros prefer to coat bare wood with oil-based primer, no matter what type of top coat they will be applying.

Latex primers are fairly tolerant of vapor drive. There are two disadvantages to using latex primers: latex-primed surfaces sometimes require an extra top coat, and latex primers sometimes allow rust stains from nailheads to show through the finish paint (Yes, even if a builder uses hot dipped galvanized nails on exterior surfaces, the rust-resistant coating takes a beating from hammers and

Clean surfaces before painting. A pressure washer can clean off a wall in a hurry. It can also help remove loose paint, although cleanup is difficult with this method.

Protect shrubs, plants, and garden ornaments with heavy canvas drop cloths. Use rocks or bricks to keep the drop cloths in place.

nail guns.) If the wood is unpainted, or if rust stains show through, spot-prime nailheads with an oil- or shellac-based primer.

Metal Primers. Most people think that ferrous metals, such as iron and steel, and commonly used flashings, such as terne and galvanized steel, can be painted, but that aluminum and copper do not require painting. It is true that ferrous metals (coated metal such as terne metal and galvanized steel) have to be painted. However, aluminum corrodes if it is left unpainted. It lasts longer and looks better when painted. Copper does not rust if left unpainted, but the greenish runoff from copper roofing and flashing stains surfaces below. Painting the copper takes care of this problem.

Ferrous Metal Primers. Ferrous metal is iron-bearing metal, that is, iron and steel. Galvanized steel, commonly used for gutters and flashings, is a ferrous metal. There are three types of ferrous metal primers: bright metal primer, rusty metal primer, and rust converters. Use bright metal primer for new metal, or for newly prepped metal that has been sanded to remove rust. Use rusty metal primer if the metal is rusted.

Terne Metal. The material that most people call "roofing tin" is actually terne metal. Terne (French for "dull") is steel covered with a combination lead and tin coating. Terne has been used as a roofing and flashing material for hundreds of years. Properly painted, it can easily last decades. However, improperly painted, it self-destructs. Coatings such as roofing tar and aluminum paint actually hasten the destruction of the metal, showing some surface rust. Of course, all loose rust has to be removed with a wire brush before the metal is painted. Rust converters promote a chemical reaction that arrests rusting, but they cannot work miracles. Very rusty metal needs replacing because no paint will help.

Before priming galvanized steel, wipe it down with mineral spirits to remove the factory-applied coating of oil. Then use a primer specifically suited to galvanized steel.

Never use aluminum paint (the shiny silver stuff) on ferrous metals. Aluminum-to-steel contact sets up galvanic corrosion, which slowly destroys the ferrous metal.

Aluminum Primers. Aluminum is primed with a metal primer or an oil-based zinc chromate paint. Top coat aluminum with ordinary latex house paint. If you are painting aluminum gutters, make sure there is no standing water left inside. Gutters that require painting need to be painted on the inside too.

Priming Basics

1. Prime new wood and any repaired sections before applying the top coats. Brush primer in the direction of the wood grain for best results.

2. The exposed edges of clapboard require primer as well. Turn the brush and flex the bristles. Complete an entire section, such as between windows, before moving to the next.

Painting

As a general rule, the faster the primer dries, the sooner you have to paint. No primer does its job if it is left exposed indefinitely. If the primer is allowed to weather beyond a critical point, it will fail or it will cure so hard that the top coat cannot stick to it. Read the manufacturer's label specifications for the optimum time between priming and applying the top coat. With some primers, you can recoat in a matter of hours. With others, you can wait a few weeks. Whatever you do, do not prime in the spring and plan to finish painting in the fall. You will end up redoing the entire job.

Painting Sequence

Circumstance has a lot to do with determining your painting sequence, but personal preference plays a role, too. For example, on summer days you will want to plan a strategy that keeps you out of the sun. If you are right-handed, work from left to right. If you are left-handed, work from right to left.

Working from the Top Down. When painting outside, work from the top down. There are two reasons for this. The first is the standing construction trade rule about "doing the hard work first." So paint from ladders and scaffolds when concentration is best and

Ladder hooks keep a can of paint where you can reach it while you are working on a ladder.

Work from the top down. That way any paint that drips to lower areas can be smoothed out or cleaned up when you reach the area. Note the incline of the ladder here and the comfortable working position it affords.

before fatigue sets in. Second, paint drips down, so you can remove drips as you proceed with the job.

Working Horizontally. When working across the face of a wall, apply paint to natural break points. For example, finish off a whole window surround before moving to the next window, or work to the end of a wall before taking a break. Plan your workday so that you make it to a break point before quitting time.

When working on a ladder, never try to scoot the ladder over as you stand on it. Always climb down and move the ladder to the next area, making sure the ladder is stable and level before going back up.

Saving Steps. Plan the order of work so that you keep the need to move ladders, drop cloths, and your painting supplies to a minimum. For example, if painting a gable wall, paint the trimwork first. Then paint the main part of the wall.

Painting Downstairs Doors and Windows. Plan your work so you paint downstairs doors and windows early in the day. That way, they will be dry at the end of the workday, allowing you to reinstall hardware and lock up ground floor doors and windows at night.

Painting Siding

Lay paint on the face of the siding, covering as large an area as you can brush out before the paint starts to pull. Brush the paint out using horizontal strokes (on shingles brush vertically along with the grain of the wood). Keep a "wet edge" and work to a logical stopping point. Drips often form on the bottom edges of siding, so be sure to look back over the work from time to time to pick up any drips or runs.

Painting Siding

1. If you need to work on a lower section first, be prepared to brush out any drips that occur later. Paint clapboard in horizontal sections.

2. Work in small sections to ensure maximum coverage of the paint. Always work toward a wet edge. Never set a brush into wet paint because it will leave a mark.

Painting Plywood and Grooved Siding. Paint Texture-1-11 (T-1-11) plywood siding using a long nap roller. Use a brush for cutting in (painting areas where the roller does not reach or where you want a sharply defined color change). Keep the brush handy as you roll on the paint. Switch to the brush frequently, brushing paint evenly into vertical grooves.

Painting Brick. Do not paint brick unless it has already been painted. Unlike wood, brick does not need to be painted to survive the weather. There is one exception to this rule: brick that has been sandblasted. In this case, paint the brick using latex to prevent water from seeping into the walls.

In fact, brick survives best unpainted because the hard face of the brick is tougher than paint, and paint tends to trap moisture in the mortar. Once brick is painted, you are stuck with the ongoing maintenance of keeping it painted. If the brick is dirty, have it cleaned.

Even the dirtiest brick can be cleaned so it looks brand new. Cleaning brick often costs less than painting it, and the cleaning lasts a lot longer than a paint job. Brick by itself requires cleaning only once every fifty years. The best contractor for the job is one who has experience cleaning older buildings.

Before painting brick, have cracks repointed (re-mortared in spots). Apply latex paint with a long-nap roller, switching frequently to a brush to work paint into the mortar joints. Check the work frequently, and pick up runs or drips. The above information applies to concrete block as well.

Painting Stucco. Stucco is painted using latex paint applied with a long-nap roller. However, unlike siding and other surfaces with many plane changes, stucco is an ideal surface for spraying if you have an airless sprayer. Cut in corners with a brush; then spray.

Patch any cracks or bulges in stucco before repainting. Make sure there are no cracks in windows and door sills, or coping that allow water to penetrate the stucco. If cracks are present, patch with stucco or a caulk that can be painted.

Painting Grooved Siding

1. Paint grooved vertical siding using a roller. Simply apply paint following the pattern of the siding.

2. Fill grooves in the siding using a thin brush. Work in small sections so that you can switch from roller to brush quickly.

Apply primer to any patched areas before painting. This is important because patches that have not been primed have different textures and absorption rates and cause an obvious change of gloss in the finish paint.

One Coat or Two? Some paints, typically higher-quality paints, are marketed as one-coat paints. Surely, the idea of one-coat paint has its attractions. One coat requires half as much material and half as much time. However, you cannot always count on paint to provide good results with just one coat. First of all, you do not want one thick coat of paint. A coating that is too thick does not cure and adhere properly. Secondly, if you are painting over a dark color with a light color, it is almost guaranteed that you will need two coats of paint to properly cover the darker color.

For a first-time paint job on raw wood or siding, apply a primer coat and two top coats. However, if you are repainting a house in a color similar to the existing color, one coat may provide perfectly acceptable results.

With older houses, consider limiting the paint job to one coat, even though it might not last as long as a two-coat job. The more coats of paint on the house, the more likely the paint is to peel. Eventually, built-up paint reaches a "critical mass," and starts to come off in chunks. Moving parts such as doors and windows bind as paint builds up. Sometimes, a little bit of paint can be the difference between an operational door and a door that sticks shut. Finally, too much paint obscures detail. Fancy moldings on older houses often lose detail because of thick layers of paint.

Staining as an Alternative. Stain is a good alternative to paint for houses that are clad with solid wood such as redwood, cedar, or cypress. It allows the wood grain to show and provides a handsome natural finish. Stains are available in latex and oil-based formulations. Both work well. Stains are essentially thinned paint, and they are available in varying opacities, from clear to nearly opaque. Stains penetrate wood more than paint, but because paint forms an outer film on the wood, it provides better protection from the weather.

A stained house requires more maintenance than a painted house. The coating has to be renewed more often. Plus, old stain does not peel like old paint. Instead, it wears away, leaving the wood exposed to the weather. Heat and humidity are tough on coatings, and even tougher on exposed wood.

Paint stucco using a long-nap roller. The long naps hold more paint than a smooth nap and it does a better job of covering the textured surface of the stucco. As with any paint job, repair all damaged surfaces before painting. Cut in around windows and trimwork using a brush.

special projects

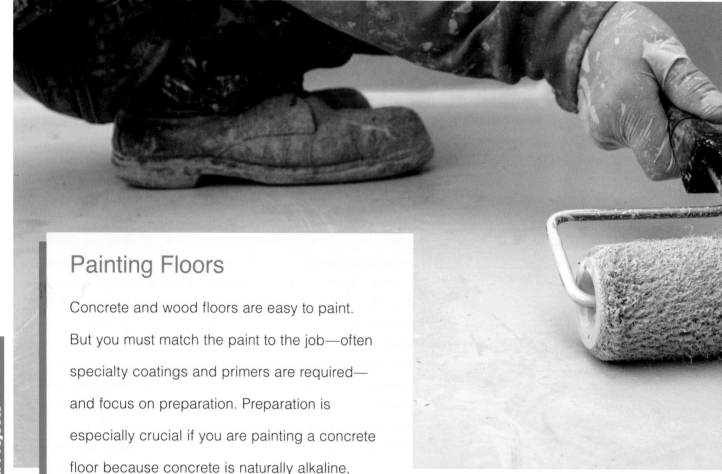

Painting Floors

Concrete and wood floors are easy to paint. But you must match the paint to the job—often specialty coatings and primers are required—and focus on preparation. Preparation is especially crucial if you are painting a concrete floor because concrete is naturally alkaline, which can degrade paint, and any moisture that comes through the concrete will cause the paint to peel in no time at all.

If you have a house that is under 20 years old, the floor may have a vapor retarder beneath it, which will prevent moisture from permeating through the floor. If you don't have a vapor retarder, as evidenced by damp or wet concrete, you may not be able to paint the floor. However, if the concrete is dry and clean (or you can clean it with some prep work), you can paint the concrete with confidence.

Garage floors must stand up to grease, grime, and heat from tires. Garage-floor painting kits can add protection and a decorative touch to the area.

Prepping and Painting Concrete Floors. The concrete surface must be clean of dust, grit, and any loose paint. Anything that gets between the paint and the concrete will block the binder, very much the way dust will defeat the sticking action of a piece of tape. Use a shop vac and make repeated passes over the floor. Seal cracks with specialty caulks that are made for concrete, such as paintable chimney repair caulk or concrete repair caulk. Larger cracks of more than ¼ inch will need to be repaired with a concrete patch kit, which often comes in the form of a two-part epoxy-type kit. Do not use caulk or spackle made for wood or plaster walls. Also, avoid using raw silicon. It will adhere to the concrete, but it isn't paintable.

Clean the concrete of efflorescence using a 10-percent solution of muriatic acid. Wear rubber gloves and eye protection when working with muriatic acid. Mop the acid solution up and let the floor dry; rinse it again. Then, wash the floor with detergent and water; rinse; and allow to dry.

Paint Choices. There are some latex-based masonry paints. They offer the same benefits as latex wall paint, including soap and water clean-up. They can also tolerate some moisture in the concrete. Epoxy paints formulated for concrete floors are your next step up in durability and price. They are a good choice for consistently moist environments. One system for garage floors consists of two parts. First you apply an epoxy paint; then you sprinkle color paint chips into the paint. This provides extra traction for the floor.

Applying Paint. If using a floor-painting kit, be sure to follow directions for surface prep. Use a thick-napped roller to paint concrete, so lots of paint gets on the floor surface. Use an extension handle so you can apply some pressure to the roller. A second coat is a must. But wait the entire dry time recommended by the manufacturer. It may take longer for paint to dry on concrete than on wood.

Painting Wood Floors

Wood floors are particularly easy to paint, though you have to determine the existing finish on the floor before you paint. If your floor is bare wood, you are in good shape. The floor can be primed and painted with ease. If the floor has a polyurethane or other type of sealing finish, such as linseed oil or teak oil, you may have to have the floor stripped before you paint. The reason for this is because the urethane or oil finish blocks the ability of the new paint to bind directly with the wood, and the paint will soon peel. If you are facing a polyurethane finish, which is really a form of plastic, just painting over it would be like applying paint to clear sandwich wrap. Paint won't be absorbed, nor will it bind to the surface.

When painting floors, be sure to remove all loose paint. A pad sander does a good job. Also, repair all nicks and gouges in the floor before painting.

Prep work makes or breaks a paint job on a floor. Any rough spots on the floor will broadcast through the paint, so don't depend on the paint to act as a filler. Also, dust and grit will show through the paint. Vacuum the floor thoroughly, and use a tac cloth to pick up dust and dirt. A tac cloth is cheese cloth soaked in varnish, and it is designed specially to pick up dust and dirt.

Bare wood floors should be primed and knotholes sealed, just as you seal them when painting knotty trim. Oil paints tend to work best for painting floors because of their relatively high durability. For high-traffic areas, apply three coats of clear polyurethane over the painted finish.

Finishing Cabinets

Painting or staining wood cabinets is no different than painting wood trim anywhere else in your house. There is no special paint, though oil-based gloss paint is more durable and washable than other types. The challenges are removing obstacles like shelves and hardware, and following a pattern that will allow you to paint a surface and leave it undisturbed as you "back out" of the cabinet to finish the job. Candidly, the best way to paint cabinets is to spray them. But you need to practice on some test surfaces to get the hang of the sprayer. It is very easy to apply too much paint, and if you do that, you'll have a mess on your hands.

Prep cabinets the way you would prep any other wood by carefully cleaning and sanding the surfaces. If there are gaps at the corners because of drying wood, use a paintable caulk to seal them. Remove all hardware, shelving, and drawers. Consider removing the doors, which you can paint or stain away from the cabinets and replace later.

Special Tools. Look for a thin, long-handled roller, often called a Johnny Roller. For paint brushes, cut the handle down, so there's just a stub by the ferrule.

Then follow a pattern, and stick to it. There are lots of patterns that will work. The goal is to paint the inside of the cabinet first, and then paint the outer surfaces.

Before applying paint, vacuum dirt and dust from the floor. It is also a good idea to wipe down the area with a damp cloth. Allow the floor to dry.

Use a roller attached to an extension pole. Apply paint in the direction of the wood grain.

Remove cabinet doors when painting or staining them.

Finishing Decks

Wood decks require some sort of finishing treatment—either paint, stain, or a clear protective coating.

High quality wood decks are usually not painted. The wood used on these surfaces, such as redwood or an imported hardwood, is too beautiful to cover with paint. Pressure-treated wood, however, can be painted. There is nothing in the wood treatment that prevents paint from binding with the wood. However, the manufacturing and treatment process depends on water, and often the treated wood is wet when you purchase it. It should be allowed to dry thoroughly. For good measure, clean it with a diluted soap and water solution using a soft brush, and allow the wood to dry thoroughly. For paint, use an exterior latex house paint.

Applying a water-repellent sealer is an annual maintenance chore. Roll, brush, or spray the sealer onto the deck.

Stains add some color to decks. Semitransparent stains allow the natural grain of the wood to show through.

Solid color, or opaque, stains help protect the wood against damage from the UV rays of the sun.

Stains. Alternatives to paint include semitransparent and opaque stains. They are not as thick as paint and are absorbed by the wood, yet they contain pigments that can thoroughly color the wood, especially if used in multiple coats. Look for stains that have UV protection because some stains not only color the wood, they can act as a wood preservative as well. When applying stains, always keep a wet edge because a distinct line will be evident where two different coats meet. Work in full board lengths, rather than in multiboard sections. When applying the stain, do not let it puddle. Apply it until the wood stops absorbing it; then brush out the excess to a new section of wood. Experiment with applying the material because you can deepen or lighten the shade of the stain by applying more or less of the material. It pays to practice on scrap lumber or in an out-of-the-way section of deck.

Water-Repellent Sealers. These products prevent the wood from absorbing moisture. Even pressure-treated lumber needs a water-repellent sealer for protection. Some sealers contain preservatives that retard decay and keep the wood from drying out, which can reduce checking, warping, and splinters. These preservatives are as thin as water, and you can brush, roll, or spray them on the deck. They do need to be applied yearly for maximum protection. When applying sealants, be sure to treat the end grain of each board and really slop it on around nails and screws.

5 Special Projects

Painting Fences

Before you paint a fence, check with your local zoning laws or neighborhood color covenants to make sure you are painting it an allowable color. You may be surprised by the rules that apply to you, especially if you want to paint the fence something other than white.

For paint, use a top-of-the-line acrylic exterior house paint. Because painting fences is so time consuming, and because the multiple surface areas of the fence won't hold paint as well as a wide consistent surface area of a wall, you want to apply a paint that will last a long time.

Prep the fence the way you would prep exterior trim. Seal knots and the heads of fasteners, especially if the fence builder didn't use galvanized or stainless-steel fasteners.

Applying Paint. The best way to paint a fence is to spray it. But setting up the drop cloths is a challenge. They must be slipped under the pickets and cut to fit around the fence posts. Even given these challenges, spraying is still the fastest way to paint the fence. But spraying paint is a difficult process to control. If you are not familiar with the spraying rig, practice in a low-profile area. A beginner usually applies too much paint. Most people rely on a number of different-size brushes to paint fences.

PRO TIP

To keep shrubs away from the fence during painting, use a piece of plywood as a shield. Slip it in behind between the shrubs and the fence; move it back to give yourself room to work when painting that side of the fence. Leave the plywood in place until the paint dries to keep the leaves and branches from scratching the finish.

Before painting, make any necessary repairs to the fence. For picket fences, use a variety of brush sizes to efficiently cover the different surface areas.

Paint solid fences and wind screens as you would any wall. Exterior latex paints do a good job on all types of fences.

Painting Metal

The trick to painting metal is to learn the three Ps: prep, prime, and paint. The prep is crucial, because if the metal surface has loose flakes, they will eventually fall off and take the new paint with them. The primer enhances the binding ability of the paint, and the paint you choose must be matched to the kind of metal being painted.

There are two common kinds of metal you are likely to encounter when painting: ferrous and galvanized. Ferrous metals are things like wrought iron rails and banisters, as well as decorative wrought landscape pieces. Galvanized metals are steel metals coated with zinc.

Ferrous Metals. Though stainless steel is ferrous, it will not rust, because of its factory stainless treatment. But other ferrous metals—sheet steel and wrought iron—will rust. Rust is nothing more than oxidation as the metal reacts with oxygen and water. To stop rusting, you need to apply

a paint to the metal that will act as a barrier to water. But that barrier must be applied to a rust-free surface, or the oxidation will proceed beneath the paint as soon as it is applied.

Prep ferrous metals by aggressively removing loose rust from the metal. Use a power tool if possible, or a wire wheel loaded onto a drill/driver. Also use wire brushes, large and small, to remove the rust. If you use sandpaper, pick an aluminum-oxide paper. If you have access to compressed air, blow the dust away and then wash the surface with soapy water before painting. If you are cleaning up new ferrous metal, note that the surface may contain oil. Remove the oil with soapy water; rinse well; and allow to dry.

Priming Ferrous Metal. As soon as the metal is dry, prime it. Apply top-of-the-line rust-inhibiting metal primer. Spare no expense here, because the amount of time you have devoted to prepping, and the hassle of re-prepping and re-painting are

worth a few extra bucks spent on paint. The primer will not only give the paint something to bind to, but it will serve to protect the metal from oxidation as well. It is recommended that you apply two coats of primer. Zinc-chromate epoxy and alkyd primers are the best.

Painting Ferrous Metal. Use a top-of-the-line acrylic latex paint. Apply it in multiple coats. With metal, you don't have the same challenges presented by the shrinking and movement of wood, so one or two coats should do the job.

Galvanized Metal. Galvanized metals are not particularly good surfaces to paint, so if you can avoid applying paint, do so. It is widely recommended that galvanized metal not be painted with oil-based paint. Instead, use a corrosion-resistant primer and acrylic, latex, or vinyl latex finish paint. There are specialty metal paints for galvanized surfaces, so ask at your paint store.

Remove rust from any metal item you plan to paint. With the loose rust gone, apply the correct primer before painting.

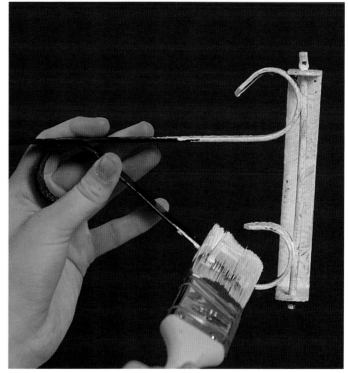

If possible, remove the metal item before you prep, prime, and paint it. You will find you have more control over the process, and you won't get paint on nearby surfaces.

cleanup & storage

Brushes and Rollers

The techniques for washing, combing, and spinning brushes are the same for latex and oil-based paints. The main difference is you can work with running water in a sink or bathtub when cleaning up after a latex paint job, but you will need turpentine or paint thinner when working with oil-based, or alkyd, paints.

Brushes. Wipe as much paint off the brush as possible before running water over it. It is okay to wash water-thinned latex paint down the drain, but you do not want to clog the drain with thick gobs of paint. Keep the water running to clear the drain during cleaning. To speed the process, add a little dish washing liquid to the water. Do the final rinse with warm water only—no soap.

If using an oil-based paint, dip the brush in a bucket containing paint thinner. Tap the bristles against the sides and bottom of the bucket to loosen the paint. Wear heavy rubber gloves while working.

1 Comb the Brush. After cleaning the brush, comb the bristles with a clean wire brush or brush comb (available at most paint and hardware stores). Do not tease the bristles. Instead, comb from the ferrule toward the tips of the bristles. The idea is to return the bristles to their original form—straight and parallel with one another.

2 Wrap the Brush. Brushes are wrapped to ensure that the bristles retain their shape as they dry. For convenience, save the stiff paper wrapper that comes with the brush. It can be replaced easily, and it fastens in place. If you have lost the wrapper, wrap the brush in newspaper or butcher paper, and secure the paper with a rubber band.

3 Store the Brush. It is best to store a brush by hanging it from the handle. Brushes can be stored flat, but do not stack or push them against other items. If the bristles are crimped or distorted during storage, they will never straighten out.

Checking the Brush. When you get ready to use the brush again, check that the bristles are soft, supple, and straight—just like new. If the bristles are stiff, but can be easily broken apart, you did not get the brush clean enough, but it can still be used. If the bristles are stuck together and will not come apart, the brush was stored dirty and is essentially useless. Do not try to paint with it. If the bristles are distorted, use the brush only for non-critical applications, such as applying paint remover or dusting before painting.

1 Use a brush comb to remove paint from the bristles. Dip the bristles in the appropriate solvent before using the brush. They work with both latex and oil-based paints.

2 Dry the brush by shaking out as much moisture as possible. Do this outside or into the tub of a utility sink. Then wrap the brush until it is completely dry. Wrap in the original wrapper or use newspaper or brown butcher's paper.

3 Many people leave the brush wrapped until it is needed again, but it is better to hang the brush for long-term storage. That way the bristles are in no danger of being damaged or misshapen during storage.

6 Cleanup & Storage

Roller Covers. Usually it is more trouble than it is worth to clean and store a roller cover. However, lamb's wool and mohair covers are expensive, and are designed for repeated cleaning. The process for cleaning a roller cover is the same when using water or oil-based paint. Just remember to use paint thinner for oil-based products. Follow these steps:

1 Bleed the Paint. "Bleed" the paint out of the cover with a curved tool such as a five-in-one, shown, or wring the paint out of the cover with your hands. Then hold the roller cover under warm running water. (Soak with clean thinner if you painted with oil-based.)

2 Spin Out the Paint. To clean the cover, spin it with a pump spinner inside a bucket, or place the cover halfway onto a roller frame and spin it. Repeat Step 1 until runoff from the cover is clear and clean.

Store the roller cover on end until it is completely dry. Try to let the cover dry without anything pressed against it, as this may cause depressions in the nap. When the cover is completely dry, store it in a clean plastic bag, or wrap it in newspaper or butcher paper.

1 If you are going to clean a roller cover, try to remove as much paint from the cover as possible. Use a putty knife or five-in-one tool to scrape paint from the surface. You can reuse this paint.

2 Clean the cover by spinning it inside a 5-gal. bucket. You can buy paint and roller spinners where paint supplies are sold. If you can't spin, hold the cover under running water to work the paint out.

Tips for Cleaning Oil-Based Paint Tools

To clean up oil paint, you will need rubber gloves, eye protection (safety glasses or goggles), rags, a wire brush, a gallon of paint thinner, and a paintbrush spinner (optional, but very useful). All of these materials are available at most paint and hardware stores.

■ Pour several inches of thinner into a used paint bucket. Then with a brush that you used for the paint job, wipe any paint off the sides and bottom of the bucket. This not only cleans the bucket, it begins the process of cleaning the brush. When the bucket is clean, pour the used thinner into any roller pan you plan to clean, and pour fresh thinner into the clean bucket. When finished, pour the used thinner into a glass jar with a lid. Let the sediment settle to the bottom. This will take a week or longer. You can reuse the clear thinner. Dump the sediment out onto newspaper, and let it dry thoroughly outside. The dry sediment, which no longer contains hazardous compounds, can be discarded with the regular trash.

■ When cleaning brushes, let the brush soak in a bucket of fresh thinner for a few minutes. Then use the wire brush to "comb" the sides and edges of the paintbrush from the ferrule toward the end of the bristles, forcing the paint out. Paint will be trapped inside the bristles near the ferrule, so repeat the process while dipping the brush into the thinner.

■ Spin the brush into a large bucket. You can also spin the brush by hand.

■ Using a clean wire brush or brush comb, reshape the bristles. When the bristles are straight and parallel, wrap the clean brush in the original wrapper or in butcher paper.

■ Leave paint- and thinner-soaked rags outside to dry. Do not bundle and store rags: they can catch fire spontaneously! When rags are thoroughly dry, dispose of them in the regular trash.

PRO TIP

Rusty tools can be reconditioned by sanding them with a palm sander. This is especially true of scrapers and knives. Just sand them with some 120-grit paper.

Shellac and Lacquer. Some coatings, such as shellac-based primers, must be cleaned up with alcohol. Lacquer must be cleaned with lacquer thinner. Working with alcohol, lacquer thinner, or other solvents requires that you wear rubber gloves and eye protection. Such solvents are highly flammable. Be careful not to open them near pilot lights and other flames. Read the label directions for the right cleaning agent and for safety precautions. In general, it is best to use disposable brushes for shellac, as the paint dries very quickly and cleans up only with chemicals.

Cleaning Other Tools. Roller pans, scrapers, putty knives, and all other painting tools are cleaned with water or the appropriate solvent and stored in a cool, dry place. Why a cool, dry place? Because metal parts rust when stored in hot, humid areas. Make sure all tools are thoroughly dry before storing them. Wet spots tend to rust during storage. To guard against rust, apply a thin coating of machine oil.

When you retrieve the tools for the next paint job, check for rust. Do not use a roller pan that has rust in places that contact the roller cover. If the tools were coated with oil before storage, wipe them down with mineral spirits to remove oil before using them again.

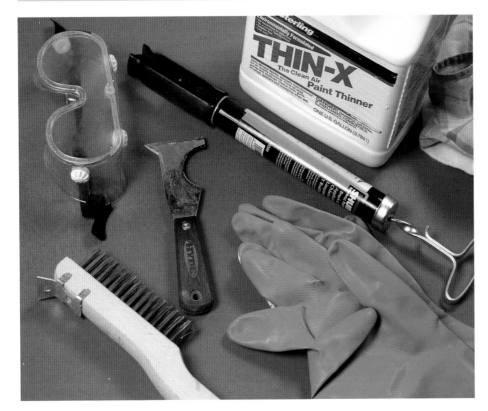

Oil-based cleanup is messy and potentially dangerous. When working with paint thinner, wear goggles and rubber gloves.

Cleaning Drips & Spills

If you get a drop of oil-based paint on a smooth finished surface, it is best to let the paint dry, then pop the paint off with a razor blade. Drips of latex paint can be wiped up while still wet. Use a damp cloth.

If you find dried drips of latex, use a proprietary cleaning solvent. If you spill a significant amount of paint on carpet or upholstery, call a professional carpet and upholstery cleaner. There is a chance the fabric can be saved. Very small drips often can be shaved off the carpet with a razor blade.

Storing Paint

Flammable solvents are best stored in a locked metal cabinet, preferably in an outbuilding. Do not store flammable materials in an area where there is a chance fumes could be ignited by the pilot flame of a water heater or furnace.

After the job is finished, keep some paint on hand for touch-ups, and for matching the paint in future paint jobs. Keep the paint labels—if colors are discontinued, a paint store can often match paints from the information on the label. If only a small amount of paint is left in a can, it will likely dry out. Pour the paint into a smaller container. Paint stores might have quart cans available. If not, a glass jar suitable for canning vegetables does the job.

Obviously staged to make a point: painting products are flammable. Never store paints, stains, or caustic solvents near open flames. Place materials in locked, ventilated cabinets.

To accelerate the drying process for latex paint, pour old paint into a box of sawdust or kitty litter. When it's completely dry, dispose of the saw dust or kitty litter in the household trash.

Storing Paint Cans. If the rim of the can is clogged with dried paint, remove the paint with an old screwdriver. Do not worry if some dried paint falls into the can, just strain the paint before you use it. Place the lid on the can. Then cover the lid with newspaper or a piece of cloth. The cloth prevents splatters. Tap the lid into place using a rubber mallet. If you do not have a rubber mallet, tap lightly on a piece of wood with a hammer. Tap all the way around the lid while listening to the sound. When the taps sound the same all the way around, the lid is firmly in place. Store latex paint where it will not freeze. If latex paint freezes, it is useless.

Seal the stored paint from contact with the air by floating a piece of plastic directly on top of the paint before sealing the lid. Some pros like to store the paint can upside down. The wet paint seals any tiny air holes. This approach avoids the "skin" that forms on paint cans stored right side up.

Disposing of Paints

Do not pour oil-based paints or thinners down the drain. Thinners and solvents in paints are hazardous materials, and dumping them down a drain ensures that they will end up in the water supply.

Laws and customs for disposal of solvents are still being created. In some areas, the local government provides a drop-off site for such materials. Some municipalities recycle the stuff as fuel for industrial furnaces. Many towns allow homeowners to let latex paint solvents evaporate into the air, then dispose of the containers in the regular trash. Check with your local recycling agency.

To save paint for later use, float a piece of clear plastic on top of the paint. Then seal the can. Drape an old towel over the lid, and tap the lid into the can groove using a rubber mallet.

6 Cleanup & Storage

resource guide

This list of manufacturers and associations is meant to be a general guide to additional industry and product-related sources. It is not intended as a listing of products and manufacturers represented by the photographs in this book.

Acme Sponge & Chamois Co., Inc.
727-937-3222
www.acmesponge.com
Distributes natural sponge and chamois products.

Arts & Crafts by Rayson
800-526-1526
www.artsandcraftsbyrayson.com
Manufactures paint supplies.

Behr
800-854-0133 ext. 2
www.behr.com
Manufactures paint, varnishes, and related products.

Benjamin Moore & Co.
800-344-0400
www.benjaminmoore.com
Manufactures paint, stains, and varnishes.

Bestt Liebco Corp.
800-523-9095
www.besttliebco.com
Manufactures painting tools, such as brushes and rollers.

California Paints
800-225-1141
www.californiapaints.com
Manufactures paint, coatings, and related materials.

Colker Company
800-533-6561
www.colkercompany.com/decorative_arts.html
Manufactures natural sea sponges and cloths.

Devine Color
503-387-5840
www.devinecolor.com
Manufactures paint and related materials.

**Devoe Paint
Ici Paints**
800-221-4100
www.icipaintsinna.com
Produces paint and related materials.

Dunn-Edwards
888-337-2468
www.dunnedwards.com
Manufactures paint and related materials.

Dutch Boy
800-828-5669
www.dutchboy.com
Manufactures paint and related materials.

Fine Paints of Europe
800-332-1556
www.finepaintsofeurope.com
Manufactures specialty paints.

General Paint
604-253-3131
www.generalpaint.com
Manufactures specialty paints.

Glidden
800-454-3336
www.glidden.com
Manufactures paint and related materials.

Golden Artist Colors, Inc.
800-959-6543
www.goldenpaints.com
Manufactures paint, varnishes, and related materials.

J.W. Etc.
361-887-6600
www.jwetc.com
Manufactures varnish, wood filler, and opaque primer.

Nour Trading Co.
800-686-6687
www.nour.com
Manufactures professional painting tools.

The Old Fashioned Milk Paint Co.
978-448-6336
www.milkpaint.com
Manufactures specialty paint.

Olympic Paints & Stains
800-441-9695
www.olympic.com
Manufactures paint, stains, and related materials.

Para Paints
905-792-0940
www.para.com
Manufactures paint, stains, and varnishes.

Pearl Paint
800-221-6845
www.pearlpaint.com
Distributes a wide range of fine-art products including
paints and brushes.

Pratt & Lambert
800-289-7728
www.prattandlambert.com
Manufactures paint, stains, and other related products.

Purdy
800-547-0780
www.purdycorp.com
Manufactures brushes and other related products.

R&F Handmade Paints, Inc.
800-206-8088
www.rfpaints.com
Manufactures paint and related materials.

Sherwin-Williams
216-566-2284
www.sherwin-williams.com
Manufactures paints and finishes.

Solo Horton Brushes, Inc.
800-969-7656
www.solobrushes.com
Manufactures artist and utility brushes.

T.J. Ronan Paint Corp.
800-247-6626
www.ronanpaints.com
Manufactures specialty paints.

U.S. Art Quest
800-200-7848
www.usartquest.com
Manufactures art supplies, including paints and adhesives.

Valspar Corp.
800-845-9061
www.valspar.com
Manufactures paint, stains, and coatings.

Werner Ladder
888-523-3370
www.wernerladder.com
Manufactures ladders and scaffolding.

Zinsser Co, Inc.
732-469-8100
www.zinsser.com
Manufactures wallcovering-removal products, primers,
and sealants.

glossary

glossary/index

Acrylic A synthetic polymer used in water-based paints. Acrylic resins act as a binder in paint.

Acrylic latex paint Water-soluble paint that contains only acrylic resin binder.

Alligatoring Paint failure condition where the paint pulls apart in a crazed line pattern that resembles alligator skin. Caused by paint applied too thickly; paint that dried too quickly; or a second coat painted over a first coat that was not dry.

Alkyds A resin used as a binder in oil-based paints.

Base coat In decorative painting this is the solid color of either gloss or semigloss paint that shows underneath the glaze coat pattern.

Binder The binder joins the pigment particles into a uniform film and binds the paint to the surface. The binder also determines the paint's washability and color retention. Look for acrylic polymers in high-performance latex paints.

Blistering Paint problem characterized by paint coming off the surface in bubbles. Caused by paint applied over a wet, oily, or dirty surface. Also occurs when water vapor escapes from the house interior.

Caulk A soft compound for sealing joints and cracks against leaks of water and air. It may be silicone or a latex synthetic compound.

Chalking Paint failure marked by a layer of fine dust on the surface of the paint. Occurs with time as weather conditions break down the paint film.

Chemical stripper A paint removing agent. Usually applied with a brush, but may be embedded in a plastic-covered poultice that is laid on a surface then pulled off.

Combing A decorative painting technique where the painter drags a comb of varying teeth width across a glazed surface.

Compressed air sprayer An electric sprayer that emits a fine mist of paint by forcing air through a paint reservoir.

Decorative painting Paint process in which a semitransparent glaze color is manipulated to create a pattern that highlights a solid base color underneath.

Dragging Creating a lined pattern in a glaze coat by pulling a brush with long bristles in overlapping vertical rows.

Drywall Also known as wallboard, gypsum board, and plasterboard; a paper-covered sandwich of gypsum plaster used for wall and ceiling construction.

Enamel A feature of paint that allows it to form a smooth surface.

Epoxy A two-part compound used to fill holes in damaged wood. Once dry, epoxy patches are very strong and can be sanded, primed, and painted.

Ferrous metal primer Specially formulated primer applied to iron-bearing metal. Commonly needed for gutters and flashing.

Flashing A shiny spotting effect in paint sheen caused by applying wet paint over an area of dry paint.

Foam brush An 1- to 4-inch, taper-edged foam pad on a stick used for applying stain and painting window muntins.

Glaze Opaque, gel-like "paint" used for decorative painting, can be water- or oil-based.

Ladder jack A plank-scaffold support arm resembling a shelf bracket. A pair of these arms (usually made of aluminum) attach to the rungs of two ladders to support an aluminum plank-scaffold.

Latex paint Paint that uses water as the vehicle to spread on, and adhere to a surface. Comes in all sheens (flat to high gloss enamel). Favored for quick drying time, easy water cleanup, and environmental safety.

Methylene chloride A chemical compound thought to be carcinogenic. Contained in most effective chemical strippers.

Mildewcide Chemical contained in paint that prevents mildew from growing.

Muntins Strips that separate window panes. On older windows muntins hold glass in place; on many newer windows they are decorative.

Natural bristles Also called "China bristles." Brush bristles from animal hair (usually hog). Use this type for oil-based paint only.

Oil paint Type of paint that uses either natural oil (such as linseed oil) or a synthetic oil (called alkyd) as the spreading and adhering vehicle. Alkyd paints are the most prevalent oil paint. Oil-based paint requires mineral spirits or turpentine to clean and thin.

Palm sander A small electric sander with a vibrating pad to which sandpaper is clamped. Shaped to fit a palm, this tool facilitates woodwork sanding.

Paperless drywall Drywall that has a fiberglass mat on its face rather than paper. It is designed this way for mold resistance.

Peeling Paint failure where paint falls off the surface. Peeling is caused by moisture problems and expansion of the painted surface.

Power roller A device that pumps paint either directly from a can or from an integrated reservoir into a roller cover. Eliminates the need to continually reload a roller cover when rolling a surface.

Primer An essential undercoat layer of paint. Primer kills stains, retards moisture absorption, and provides a good surface for a top coat of paint to adhere. Primer comes in water- and oil-based formulas. It is imperative that new or bare wood and metal be primed.

Propulsion sprayer Machine that spits or "flips" small droplets of paint. Paint is supplied by either an attached reservoir or drawn from a paint can. With an adjustable rate of spray mist and pressure these machines are excellent for spraying large surfaces.

Rag rolling Process of rolling a loosely wound rag down a glazed surface in vertical columns. Creates a soft, repetitive pattern.

Ragging Decorative paint process using a bunched-up rag to remove glaze and create a mottled pattern with the underneath base color.

Roller cover Cylindrical cover used over a roller handle to roll paint onto a surface. Available in varying nap thicknesses for specific tasks and made of either nylon, lamb's wool, or foam.

Rotary disk sander Hand-held machine to which an abrasive sanding disk is attached to remove large areas of paint on flat surfaces.

Rough-surface painter A combination brush and paint pad, this tool is useful for painting rough shingles and masonry. Short bristles resemble a scrub brush.

Sash brush A finely bristled brush with an angled taper that makes sharp lines on trim, molding, and window muntins.

Sash The framework into which window glass is set. Double-hung windows have an upper and lower sash.

Scaffolding Connected metal sections with lumber planks, or an aluminum plank spanning two ladder jacks used as an elevated work platform.

Sheen The degree of gloss in a paint. Sheen ranges from flat to high gloss.

Sponging Using a natural sea sponge, or synthetic sponge with ripped edges, that is dipped in colored glaze to apply decorative finish on a solid base coat.

Stain brush A short and wide bristled brush used for stain. The bristles reduce the amount of stain that runs into the brush ferrule.

Stippling Process of gently removing a glaze coat with the fine bristles of a stippling brush.

Trisodium phosphate (TSP) A strong powdered cleaning agent to be mixed with water and used to clean house exteriors and walls that have remaining wallpaper glue.

VOC (Volatile Organic Content) Any carbon compound that evaporates at room temperature. Nearly all solvents (except water) are VOCs. Many states limit the amount of VOCs that can be found in paint.

Volume solids Always expressed as a percentage, this is the volume of pigment and binder divided by the total volume of paint. High-volume solids result in a paint with a thicker film and better durability.

Wet edge The leading working edge of a coat of wet paint.

index

index